Macclesfield
Hall of Fame

Published by Sigma Leisure – an imprint of
Sigma Press, Stobart House, Pontyclerc, Penybanc Road
Ammanford, Carmarthenshire SA18 3HP

British Library Cataloguing in Publication Data

A CIP record for this book is available from the British Library

ISBN: 978-1-85058-900-6

Typesetting and Design by: Sigma Press, Ammanford, Carms

Cover photographs:
front: left to right (from top): John Mayall, Peter Crouch, Professor Sir James Chadwick, Helen Atkinson Wood, Terence Hardy Waite, Reg Harris statue in Manchester Veladrome, Rt Hon Sir Alan James Beith, Nick Robinson and Jamie Donaldson
back: left to right: England cricket cap, Olympic gold medal Seoul 1988, England soccer cap France 1983-84 and Commonwealth cricket team touring badge 1953-54

Printed by: Bell & Bain Ltd, Glasgow

Macclesfield
Hall of Fame

Bob Burrows

Thanks to wife Pat, my computer brain, and to son Nik and daughter Penny, who like me grew up in Macclesfield and have given us the joy of a granddaughter Emily and a grandson Jacob.

Contents

About the Author

Bob Burrows has resided in Macclesfield for 65 years. He grew up living in Waters Green, Pierce Street, Chester Road, Weston council estate and Byrons Lane. Together with his education, firstly at Christ Church primary school, then Park Royal Secondary where he was Head Boy and finally, in 1956 at the age of fifteen, King's School, where he met several of the characters featured in the book, he is well qualified to write of his home-town. He is a past-chairman of Macclesfield Forest Round Table in 1974 and he also spent more than twenty years playing soccer and cricket in the local and Cheshire leagues.

An Associate of the Institute of Banking, he started his career as a junior clerk in Macclesfield. Despite refusing to move from his Macclesfield home, he earned several promotions and experience in Derby, Manchester and Liverpool, before retiring as Area Director for the north-west based in Liverpool. Following his retirement, he took up writing as a hobby and to date has had seven books published, together with more than 100 articles in magazines and newspapers.

His family comprises wife Pat, married son Nik with daughter Emily, married daughter Penny with son Jacob.

Introduction

For a town of its size Macclesfield has made an astonishing contribution to the history and social culture of Great Britain. Its citizens have excelled in the arts, military, science, politics, business, music, literature, media, sport and show business.

This book features those Maxonians who have achieved national or international fame in their chosen field, with the qualification that they must have been born, raised, educated or spent many years in the town.

Maxonians have attained the rank of Major General, Squadron Leader and Group Commander, have been knighted and appointed Lords and Equerry to Queens Victoria and Alexandria, have been awarded the Nobel Peace Prize, the Stalin Peace Prize, the Canada Medal, the United States Medal of Merit and honoured in the Canadian Aviation Hall of Fame. Macclesfield soldiers defended Ladysmith, relieved Khartoum and excelled at the Battle of Britain. One scientist discovered the neutron, another featured in the discovery of DNA, while another is responsible for the breakthrough in a global treatment of leukaemia. A Maxonian went with Shackleton to Antarctica, one had a bridge in Africa named after him and another is today regarded as the world's leading explorer.

In sport Macclesfield citizens have won Olympic gold, played soccer for England and Northern Ireland, have won the FA Cup and League double and scored 100 runs against the West Indies. One became Head of BBC Test Match cricket, another was appointed Head Cricket Coach for England, and yet another captained England at rugby, and a Maxonian golfer actually beat Tiger Woods in a day's play in Dubai.

Macclesfield gave Britain's foremost canal engineer his grounding, was the home of the man who made the town the leader in the world's silk industry, and also educated the head of Britain's largest bank as well as educating the Dean of Canterbury. The town's politicians have been Speaker of the House of Commons, Chief Parliamentary Whip and Deputy Leader of the Liberal Party.

In the world of music Joy Division had hit records and a film made about their life, one musician was regarded as a Blues Legend and nurtured Eric Clapton, another was Britain's foremost male opera singer, starring at La Scala whilst another became the Number One Disc Jockey in Hollywood, credited with naming the 1960s cult phenomena 'flower power'. Maxonians have starred in Blackadder, featured in the country's most successful soaps and one is appearing in two of televisions top series. Two renowned writers are also popular in America and one is to have a film made of her life, in addition the town is the birthplace of the country's finest wild life painter.

Maxonians proliferate in the media; one appears on our screens most nights as the BBC's Chief Political Editor, one became Broadcaster of the Year, another was named as the European Radio Personality and yet another was appointed Controller of BBC TV before becoming Chief Executive of Channel 4, responsible for many of our most popular programmes. The town is also the birthplace of the world's longest held hostage who was later voted BBC Man of the Year.

Macclesfield is surrounded by beautiful countryside and there is easy access to rail and airport. The town has undergone considerable change over the years, successfully metamorphosing from its mill town heritage into an all embracing, diverse, thriving community. The achievements of our fellow Maxonians can only enhance the pride in our town and enforce the belief that there are very few places that can offer a more satisfying way of life.

Bob Burrows
November 2010

Macclesfield – A Brief History

History defies allocating a specific date for the founding of Macclesfield but all indications are that it was established more than a thousand years ago. Nearby Prestbury, an important area during that time, had a Saxon church believed to have dated from the eighth century.

Geographically the site of Macclesfield was an ideal location for a settlement, which originated roughly where today's Market Place is situated; on high ground, surrounded by rich forest with a dramatic drop to the River Bollin on the east and steep slopes on several sides and almost certainly fortified on the more vulnerable western side. Later in the town's history the lower reaches of the town, i.e. Waters Green, was linked to the upper levels by a series of constructions. The unique 108 Steps, Brunswick Hill and Backwallgate were all created because access, particularly in the winter months, was treacherous for cart and horse. The lower reaches were very often heavily flooded when the River Bollin overflowed its banks.

An intelligent estimate for the founding of the town suggests that a reasonably prosperous Saxon settlement, perhaps just a few huts or shelters, housing a small number of people within the fortifications, was evident around the 1040s indicated by a valuation of £8 in ancient records at the time of Edward the Confessor. However, this tiny settlement was soon destroyed when William the Conqueror, following his successful invasion of England in 1066, sent his Norman armies north to suppress rebellion. Nearby Prestbury and the surrounding villages, including Macclesfield,

108 Steps

Churchwallgate

Backwallgate

were burnt and their inhabitants slaughtered. The Domesday Book in 1086 mentioned 'Maclesfield' but listed only four serfs and valued the surviving hamlet at £1, an indication of its destruction. Following the crushing of the rebels, William gave Chester, including the small settlement of Macclesfield, to his nephew and a relatively peaceful period ensued under the protection of the Earl of Chester who assumed the title of Lord of the Manor of Macclesfield. The area was richly forested and game was in abundance, although there were stringent laws in place establishing strict limitations on hunting. Nevertheless the availability of a range of forest game complemented the growing of crops as the population started to increase. Macclesfield Forest covered a massive area and was home to wild boar, deer, hare, rabbit, game birds and wolves. But organised farming led to large areas being cleared and used for grazing for sheep and cattle as well as for crop growing.

During this time the name of the settlement had evolved to 'Makeslesfeld'.

How Macclesfield got its name is a matter of conjecture. The name of the leader of a group of Anglo-Saxons was named Macca. Arable land was known as 'field' so when the field became ploughed it was known as Maxfield later translated to Macclesfield. Others suggest that it was named after 'Michael's Field' probably named after Saint Michael. St Michael's church was built in 1278 on its present site in Macclesfield, so at the time of the Domesday survey the area would probably have been named after the field that hosted the original settlers: although there is no conclusive evidence for the naming.

Following the death of the 7th Earl of Chester in 1238 with no male heirs, the area was taken over by Henry III and the whole region became the property of the crown. The population was estimated to be around 1000.

Henry in turn gave the region to his son Lord Edward who granted Macclesfield its Royal Charter in 1261.

The Charter declared Macclesfield to be a free Borough and amongst other privileges it released the townspeople from paying taxes on bridges, roads or ferries and allowed the people's animals to use the Forest for pasturing and gave them the right to take wood to maintain their houses and fences. Edward succeeded his father to the throne in 1272. It was King Edward 1st who adopted the longbow following the defeat of the Welsh in 1284 and it was Cheshire archers who over the next two hundred years would become renowned for their expertise with this deadly weapon.

Wild game in the vast Macclesfield Forest and surrounding areas was hunted by longbow sometimes illegally, and local men became renowned for their expertise and were in demand by the English army for numerous campaigns. It is known that Edward I, the Black Prince, visited Macclesfield several times in the late 13th and beginning of the 14th century bringing with him his Queen, Eleanor. They stayed in the manor house in the 'Lords Park' – South Park today, an area situated between Park Lane and Gawsworth Road. They also had a hunting lodge that was used when they were pursuing deer in Macclesfield Forest.

During the 100 Years War with France, the Black Prince selected Cheshire knights and 100 Cheshire archers to be his vanguard. It was the skill of Cheshire archers that ensured many of the English victories and it is estimated that Macclesfield had a formidable force of some 200 archers. Richard II, Edward's son, also elected to have Cheshire archers as his personal bodyguards.

Farming and hunting and a period of stability led to the gradual development of the community. The town had a weekly market and had established an annual Barnaby Fair held on St Barnabas Day, 11th June, that is still acknowledged today, albeit in a much reduced form. The second annual fair was All Saints held on 1st November.

Macclesfield has a rich and varied history, particularly during the very early medieval period but sadly little remains in terms of buildings or structures from that time.

The expression Macclesfield Castle is somewhat of a misnomer. Situated approximately in the region of where the Castle Inn is sited off Churchwallgate, it started out as a grand mansion serving as a residence for Jordan de Macclesfield and John de Macclesfield, Mayors of the town in 1337 and 1358. However it is more regarded as the residence of the Duke of Buckingham and his family who developed the grand house into a more fortified, castellated building. Legend has it that the 'castle' was linked to St Michael's Church higher up the hill by an underground tunnel. Sadly only a couple of worn stones survive from the original castle, one bearing the date 1400.

Buckingham a powerful figure in English history, fought with the King and the Lancastrians when the War of the Roses erupted in 1455 but was wounded by an arrow in the face at the first Battle of St Albans. His son was killed in the same battle and Buckingham was himself killed in 1460 when leading the Lancastrian army to defeat at the Battle of Northampton.

Debate continues amongst the historians as to whether Macclesfield was a walled town. Several claims to locate sections of wall in various parts of the town have been complemented by those who assume that several of our town's street names which still survive, indicate 'gates', i.e. entrances to a wall, Chestergate, Jordangate, Churchwallgate. It has been postulated that during the Civil War of 1642, Oliver Cromwell,

13th century St Michael and All Angels Church

Town Hall and market place

*The Bate Hall Hotel –
Cromwell stayed here*

the leader of the victorious Parliamentarians, ordered that the 'walls' of Macclesfield be totally destroyed. Incidentally it also believed that Cromwell stayed at what is now the Bate Hall Inn, although in those times it was the home of the Parliamentarian, James Stopford.

Standing in today's Market Place or sitting in the modern very smart coffee shops gazing out onto the square and St Michael's Church, it is difficult to imagine the drama, the pageantry and the tragedies enacted in the square in front of the church since its original construction in 1278.

King Edward 1 and his wife Eleanor of Castile, visited 13th century Macclesfield on several occasions and the building of the church was inspired by Eleanor. To the right of today's building can be seen the Savage Chapel first endowed and built in 1502 by Thomas Savage, the Archbishop of York. Thomas, originally from Macclesfield, died in York and at his request his heart was returned to the town and interred in the Savage Chapel. The Savage family are commemorated in the chapel by a series of effigies.

Just between the Savage Chapel and the main tower of the church are nine windows forming part of the Legh Chapel. The Legh family were a well known and powerful local dynasty and Piers Legh, who was knighted on the battlefield after the bloody but historic British victory at Agincourt in 1415, died in Paris of wounds received later in the campaign. The Legh Chapel was built in 1422 to receive his body.

Although the church has changed and today's buildings has not existed for long, the plateau is still essentially the same that has witnessed several other historic events. Buried in the grounds of the church are the remains of Sir Piers Legh of Lyme (same family as Sir Piers of Agincourt), who had the great misfortune to be a friend and supporter of Richard II who lost his throne to the Duke of Lancaster, Henry IV in 1399. Henry regarded Legh as an enemy and had him executed, displaying his head on a pike on a turret at Chester Castle. However his body was retained by Carmelite monks and after 200 years the remains were moved and taken for burial in St Michael's, Macclesfield.

While sipping coffee, today's Maxonians or visitors gaze out at the impressive Town Hall building. For several hundreds of years the site was occupied by the old Guildhall, which was very much the centre of the town and where the Royal Bakehouse was situated. It was a communal bakehouse for the townspeople. Old drawings of the building show that it had iron railings supporting a stone staircase. Errant citizens were tied to the railings and flogged or placed in the stocks just a few yards away. In the early 1820s the Guildhall was demolished and in 1823 the present Town Hall was erected on the

Town Hall, built 1823

site. However the site was still the focal point for public punishments. The last public flogging was carried out in 1831 after the Watch Committee assumed responsibility for law and order in the town.

In the 1480s Sir John Savage assembled a force of men at arms and archers in the Market Place before marching off to fight at the Battle of Bosworth Field in 1485. Victory resulted in the death of Richard III; Sir John's son was knighted for his valour and Sir John was rewarded with land.

In 1513, Macclesfield men assembled in the Market Place to go fight and beat the Scots in the bloody Battle of Flodden Field. Their triumphant return was tarnished by the death during the battle of Macclesfield's Mayor and the loss of a considerable number of local men, some prominent, which affected the economic and social progress of the town.

However, earlier in 1502, within sight of the market place, just behind the church, Macclesfield's first school was established. Macclesfield was very fortunate to benefit from the will of an ex- Maxonian, Sir John Percyvale who had left the town and made his fortune in London. However he did not forget his hometown and through his generosity made provision for the education of Macclesfield children and Percyvale's School was established, which would later become known as King's School, one of the greatest in the north of England. The first school was situated close to St Michael's Church and overlooked what is today Sparrow Park. When I lived in Waters Green, Sparrow Park was my playground.

The town continued to prosper during the Tudor era and local people started to become more independent. It was noticeable that the areas surrounding the town such as Gawsworth, Bollington, Sutton and parts of the Macclesfield Forest were being settled and developed for farming grazing and crop growing. Land was being cultivated and sheep farming began to thrive with the result that wool started to appear in the local markets along with all the other locally produced goods. It was clear from the market stalls of the time that cottage industries were growing fast and people were bringing their wares to a vastly extending market that ran from Wallgate right down into Waters Green; harness makers, fletchers, shoemakers, glovers, wheelwrights, fine leather workers, button makers as well as butchers, bakers and fishmongers displayed and sold their goods in stalls for which they paid a rent. Trade was varied and ever increasing. With goods made at home and food and meat being produced and sold publicly there was a need for control and order. A security force was employed to ensure that standards and fair play prevailed in the method and quality of trade. Inspectors were responsible for spot-checking, fish, meat, corn, grain, bread, ale, testing the quality of hides and checking weights and measures as well as keeping law and order during crowded market days.

However tragedy was about to strike when the town was hit by the plague that started in 1602 and lasted until November 1603. Out of a population of about 3000, 130 people lost their lives; packed closely into small houses in tight communities the disease, spread by rats, was difficult to control and all efforts were made to prevent the gathering of people.

No sooner was this tragedy overcome, communities restructured and trade beginning to flourish, when politics created a storm that would affect everybody.

In 1642 the outbreak of the First English Civil War pitted local military leaders against each other (see King's School chapter) as the town was captured for the Royalists, then regained by the Parliamentarians, who successfully beat off a further attack by the Royalists.

Towards the end of the 17th century Macclesfield was a thriving market town with cattle, horses, sheep, pigs and poultry being sold or exchanged alongside wood, iron, receptacles, farm implements, cloth ribbons, tapes, fancy goods and an early appearance of locally made silk buttons, which by 1649 was a thriving well-established trade. Merchants bought the materials and women and children using needles made the buttons.

In 1660 Charles II was restored to the throne and in 1684 granted a further Charter to Macclesfield that gave the town additional privileges, one of which was to permit the conduct of water from the Common by pipe, making the town one of the first in the country to have water transported underground by pipe.

The market place, however, once again became the centre of another historic moment when it played host to alarming but colourful visitors on 1st December, 1745, when the Scottish cavalry of the Young Pretender, Bonnie Prince Charlie rode through the centre of Macclesfield and demanded to see Sir Peter Davenport. They commandeered his house in Back Street (now King Edward Street) for their leader. The foot soldiers arrived, 10000 strong, kilts swinging, bagpipes blaring, drums beating, banners waving, each contingent led by a colonel and all dressed in Highland uniforms. The Prince, Charles Edward, was in Highland dress with a blue waistcoat trimmed with silver, supported by his 40 strong bodyguard all dressed in blue. The column included fifteen cannon and fifty wagons loaded with ammunition and most of the foot soldiers carried muskets, Scottish broad-swords and some had pistols. The Mayor and the Aldermen were forced to formally proclaim the Pretender in the market place.

Before heading south two days later, the rebels took all the arms and ammunition they could find and threatened death and destruction of property if the town did not supply them with sufficient bread to feed their army.

This triumphant entrance of the Jacobite rebels was not to last. Just days later, their army in disarray, they stayed two nights in Macclesfield on their retreat north before stealing goods, food, clothing and cash from the residents.

On 10th December, hot on the heels of the rebels William, Duke of Cumberland arrived with the English army and stayed three nights in the Jordangate house of the Town Clerk, John Stafford. The name of the house was changed to Cumberland House and is still a fine

BWA woven silk picture depicting arrival of Bonnie Prince Charlie

building today. Just a few weeks later Cumberland's army slaughtered the Scots at Culloden in 1746 but Bonnie Prince Charlie escaped to France.

Although Sir Peter Davenport could hardly be blamed for the rebels taking over his house for their Prince it seems likely that he was punished for their actions. In 1746 his house was taken from him and, in 1748, converted for the use of the original Sir John Percyvale Grammar School, which was expanding rapidly. The school now named King Edward the Sixth Grammar School would later of course become known as

Cumberland House

King's School and the street was renamed King Edward street.

It was around this time in 1741 that the arrival of a young man, Charles Roe, to the town would change its face forever and make Macclesfield renowned around the world.

Roe, who in 1742 was manufacturing silk buttons, could see the benefits of a water driven new machine designed by an Italian, for throwing silk thread and doing away with the traditional hand throwing methods, so long established. He established in 1743 his first silk factory at the bottom of Mill Street close by the river at Dams Brook. Hugely successful, he was soon employing more than 350 workers and other silk mills started to spring up all around the area. Men women and children were employed in the mills and for a time it flourished. Early boom however was followed by depression created largely by foreign competition but Roe sold out his interest in the silk industry at the height of the boom. Macclesfield with its labour force and its mills was committed to the industry and it was eventually saved by the expansion in 1790 into weaving, which recreated the prosperous years. Manufacturing woven silk by highly trained staff boomed during the Napoleonic Wars when there was no competition from France and Macclesfield, around 1817, had 12 woven silk manufacturers and 28 silk throwsters.

Not long after the war further depression resulted from increased competition but picked up again in the 1820s and more than 10,000 people were employed in the silk industry in Macclesfield during this time in an estimated 70 factories. Dwellings had to be found for the rising working population and houses sprung up in packed terraces. Of course, many had no water, electricity, gas or sewage and some rules of sanitation had to be instigated to prevent disease spreading like wildfire in these closely packed communities.

The population of the town was estimated at around 4,500 in 1720 but boomed from the period 1750-1850. One figure set the population at 7,000 in 1786 but the calculation of figures was very much flawed. However in 1801 there was the first official census revealing a figure of 8743 in about 1,500 dwellings, which had doubled to a population of 16,000 by 1821. One or two outlying settlements were brought into the calculations when the borough was reconstituted in 1851 giving a population of 39,000 in an estimated 6,200 dwellings. Much house building had taken place due to the influx of workers into the silk industry and many three storied houses with a garret were built enabling the worker to use the top storey to weave silk and cotton on their hand-looms. Many of these 'weavers cottages' still exist in the town and good examples can be found in Paradise Street, Park Lane and Windmill Street. The cottages and indeed the larger grand houses were lit by candlelight or oil-lamps. After an aborted attempt at installing a gas pipe street lighting system in 1815 a much-improved system was successfully adopted in 1819. It was around this time that the more affluent people of the town, managers, manufacturers, etc started to move away from the centre of Macclesfield to the outlying areas. Many of the local shopkeepers lived on the premises but very

Frost's silk mill, built 1785   *Lomas's mill*

Macclesfield Sunday School, now Heritage Centre

many people traded via the market stalls. There was a thriving butter market outside the Town Hall around the 1820s and one statistic revealed that twelve tons of locally made cheese changed hands during one market day!

In terms of building, the 1800s saw the biggest and fastest expansion in the town's history. Sadly, for the average person, life was tough, uncertain and short lived. Indeed, shocking statistics revealed that life expectancy in 1841 was 24, which by 1854 had risen to 27! Another survey in 1851 indicated a thriving community; 122 inns and 42 pubs served the population with an estimated 800 shops, 20 private schools and several church schools for the poor. It is worthy of note that in 1814 Macclesfield Sunday School was built in Roe Street for the benefit and education of the town's poorer children. Many families took advantage of its services and it was a great source of enlightenment for the burgeoning community. The building is still in use today as the Heritage Centre. There was a diverse cross section of the populace from surgeons, lawyers, doctors, to coach builders, shoemakers, right across the spectrum. The town was developing at such a rate that it was deemed worthy of a newspaper and in 1811 the Macclesfield Courier became Macclesfield's first newspaper.

Astonishingly there was a regular and thriving transport system by coach and horses to most parts of the country setting out from such old coaching inns as the Pack Horse, Bulls Head and the Macclesfield Arms.

Passengers embarked for the journey complete with luggage, coats, hats and whatever comforts were required for the journey. At the sound of the guards bugle, the horses would be whipped into action and off they went; London was reached in twenty-four hours. The Macclesfield Arms building in Jordangate, now called King Edward House is now commercial offices but in its heyday played host to many travellers, including on 18th October, 1832 the soon to be

King Edward House, formerly Macclesfield Arms coaching inn

Queen, Princess Victoria and her mother the Duchess of Kent. However change was very much in the air and the glamorous, if arduous method of travelling by coach and horse was about to come to an end. In 1845 the railway came to Macclesfield. Massive crowds watched the first train leave Macclesfield for Manchester and return two hours later. The terminal station was located close to Beech Lane and the railway, in fact, runs virtually under my house and under my neighbour's grand old house, built in 1817, home for many years to the Vicars of Macclesfield. A new tunnel was cut under Beech Lane and the head of the tunnel is about thirty yards from my garden. It would change the travel habits of this country and sounded the death for coach building with its related industries. Macclesfield would have, until the 1960s, two railways with stations at Hibel Road and Central. Today only the Central Station, which opened in 1872, survives.

The rapid growth of the town and the presence of so many pubs and drinking places required a more structured system of law and order and after the Watch Committee was established with a handful of men in 1836 it quickly proved to be inadequate. In 1846 the town agreed a larger more powerful police force to maintain peace on the streets.

For almost 200 years the silk industry endured boom and bust but for many years Macclesfield was renowned throughout the world and was the centre of the silk industry in Britain. The Brocklehurst family took over from Charles Roe as the main proponents of the industry and John Brocklehurst, MP for the town, fought for the people and the silk industry on many occasions in the House of Commons. In 1929 the Brocklehursts joined with another local firm William Whiston to form Brocklehurst Whiston Amalgamated (BWA) and they continued to export high quality silk ties, silk handkerchiefs and scarves all over the world. Sadly, in 1992, they finally closed their doors as the silk industry declined for the last time.

For many of us Maxonians it was a proud feeling to know that our hometown was known throughout the world. It was brought home to me very graphically and unexpectedly during a holiday to China in 1992. We were visiting a silk factory in Chendge, northern China, when the guide, during his talk, paused to tell us that England had once produced the finest silk in a place called Macclesfield. I was proud, and he was astonished, when I told him that we were from Macclesfield!

The late Victorian era was a period of intense building, particularly of public building including a whole range of church buildings acknowledging the diverse denominations evident in the town. A number of the public buildings show the distinctive Gothic style of architect James Stevens. These large impressive buildings gave a feeling of permanency and solidity and gave the area character. The Cemetery was built in 1866, Parkside Hospital, which was designated the County Asylum for Cheshire in 1871, the hugely impressive Infirmary building in 1872 and the Park Green Library in 1876. In addition to these buildings was the Manchester and Liverpool Bank building on the corner of the Market Place and Brunswick Street, a superb building established in 1881 which later became the District Bank.

1871 saw the erection of the Drill Hall in Bridge Street paid for largely by public subscription. It would for the next 100 years, provide a venue for meetings of all kinds, concerts, boxing tournaments, local fairs, a variety of entertainment and for a time up until 1967 became the base of a battalion of the Cheshire Territorial Army. The building, albeit somewhat changed, still exists today.

The period from approximately 1830s through to the late 1890s was prolific in the erection of church buildings, many of them highly distinctive and a reflection of the Victorian era. The building industry boomed, not only from the creation of public buildings but also from the need for private housing to accommodate mill workers and the many new people attracted to the area. The Primitive Methodist Church was built in Beech Lane in 1830, Holy Trinity at Hurdsfield in 1837, St Alban's 1840s, St Paul's 1844 and St Peter's 1849 to name just a few and of course there were a number of churches already established in the town, prior to this growth period. A number of the organisations also offered educational facilities for children in their Sunday school programmes. However, towards the end of the century it was standard practice that children would spend half a day in school and the other half working in the mills or on looms at home. Previously the Sunday Schools had provided a source of education for the children who had to work all through the rest of the week. Social planning also realised the need for community spaces and West Park was created in 1854 with a very impressive bandstand, Victoria Park was developed in 1897 and had a superb avenue of trees and a distinctive grand bandstand; the precedent was set by John Ryle who after his death, donated park land still known today as South Park. These open spaces were vital for the townspeople crowded into small, terraced houses with little light, space or garden; the parks were packed, usually on Sundays. 1854 also saw the introduction to the town of a name now synonymous for quality service, Arighi Bianchi. Antonio Arighi and Antonio Bianchi a penniless cabinetmaker from Italy started their furniture business, which in 1883 moved to its present site with its highly distinctive exterior, on the Silk Road. The company has over the years been renowned for quality furniture and features Royalty amongst its clients.

Old photographs taken between 1890-1903 reveal a town surprisingly green. Trees are scattered amongst the streets. Iron railings protect a number of cultivated trees and there are a number of ivy-covered buildings.

Park Green in particular looked to be an elegant area with an avenue of trees and street gas lights set against a background of huge, impressive buildings; the distinctive columns of the 'Greek' styled bank building erected for the Lancashire and Yorkshire Bank in 1818 and in more modern times the home of Martins Bank, sadly empty today and falling into disrepair, stands next to the highly distinctive

Gothic style of the United Reformed Church (formerly the Congregational Chapel) still in use today. Across the road was the elegant Free Library building erected in 1876 which today is the Registrars Office and behind the area of the Cenotaph there was the Park Green Mill built around 1785, which now houses Gradus, and next to that was Frost's silk mill, a massive construction erected in 1785.

Chestergate, on old photographs, appears to be a vibrant, bustling main street full of character, shops with makeshift canopies displaying all kinds of goods, gas lamps line the street, ladies in full skirts and bonnets and men in jackets with flat caps or trilbies stroll along, while landaus, pony and trap and a range of horse carriages decorate the scene. However in the Waters Green area at the turn of the century activity is not quite so elegant when any of the twelve fairs are in full swing. The railway clearly brought many

Arighi Bianchi, established 1854

benefits and one was the ability to move large items, e.g. livestock, quickly over large distances. This made the Macclesfield Fairs and Markets even more attractive and it became easy to move Irish and Welsh ponies and horses by rail to Macclesfield. On some market days there were hundreds of horses, some untamed and unshod, allowed to run at speed along Waters Green for the benefit of prospective buyers. At a Wakes Fair in 1902 there were almost 1,700 entries of cattle and sheep!

The early 1900s brought with it a whole new concept of entertainment to Macclesfield with the advent of the cinema. From

1910 until the opening of the Majestic in 1922 the town was blessed with six cinemas. The first was the Palace, later to be named the Regal, then the little known King's Hall, the Drome, the Cinema, Premier and finally the Majestic. In my childhood I visited all, except the King's Hall. The Majestic on Mill Street with its highly individual white tiled front, topped with a white dome ,is now an integral part of the town's scenery and thank goodness was not allowed to be destroyed after closing in 1997. For many years it doubled as a cinema and a theatre and many plays, concerts and pantomimes were staged there particularly during the Second World War and helped keep spirits up. It seems very ironic that in these ultra modern days of High Tec communications and all round entertainment facilities, that the town does not posses a single dedicated cinema. Despite countless protests and promises the situation has remained so since 1997.

However, the world was soon to become embroiled in a conflict so horrific that even by the standards of history's bloody encounters would exceed them all. In 1914 the First World War commenced and the town was quickly emptied of men as they volunteered or were conscripted

top: *Chestergate with the Town Hall in the distance*
above: *Waters Green*

into the army. The carnage meant that constant replenishment of fighting men rendered many small towns virtually empty of working aged men.

Women manned the factories, ran the home and looked after the children while the men were away. Severe food shortages resulted in higher prices and long queues became the order of the day. Soon even the basic foods of the working class, bread and potatoes became scarce and coal was rationed in 1917 as the effort to maintain war supplies struck home. In 1918 the government deemed it necessary to introduce compulsory food rationing.

Surviving soldiers returned home to a town suffering severe deprivation. Wives had become independent while their men were away; children in some cases did not remember their fathers and in most cases looked to their mothers for influence

Old Majestic building

and guidance. Many of the men felt unwanted particularly as jobs were scarce.

Macclesfield paid a severe price with the loss of almost 700 citizens killed in the First World War and in 1921 the cenotaph was created in gardens in Park Green to commemorate the men who had sacrificed their lives. The names of the war dead are listed on four stone pillars in the garden. The war dead of the Second World War were added and each year the cenotaph becomes the emotional centre on Remembrance Sunday.

The bravery of Maxonians who died in the service of their country was evident in the award of three Distinguished Service Medals, six Military Medals and one Military Cross. Lieutenant Colonel Elstob from Siddington, was posthumously awarded the country's highest honour, the Victoria Cross and also received the Military Cross and the Distinguished Service Order. However to the tribulations of a post war Macclesfield was added another burden when the great flu epidemic of 1918 struck the town and lasted through to 1920. By this time there were more than 2 million men unemployed in Britain and of course the glamorous age of the 'Roaring Twenties', the 'black bottom,' dance craze and the 'flapper' era dawned but had little impact on Macclesfield and its myriad closely packed terraced houses, with their metal baths stuck on a nail on a wall at the back of the house and a yard with a single toilet shared by five houses or more, together with a water tap servicing the same number of houses. Very little glamour there!

Change though was in the air in 1927; the hairdryer, electric razor, pop up toaster, hearing aid, frozen food, television and talking movies were all invented at this time and would eventually make life a lot easier for the masses, but not just yet.

The great depression was about to take effect and huge industrial unrest across the country resulted in the General Strike of 1926. Times were hard, food was scarce and families had to scavenge for coal and basic foodstuffs. Poaching in the countryside was rife as fathers moved to desperation to feed their families, caught rabbits, hare and fish.

The silk industry however was still in operation and by the 1930s some stability had returned and the town once again enjoyed its annual Barnaby shut down at the end of June as townsfolk queued to get on the steam trains or buses to embark on their annual holidays to the seaside. It was in 1930 that the town appointed its first Silk Queen, a tradition that was to last for many years. The young lady chosen from the many young girls working in the numerous mills and factories became an ambassador for the town promoting the silk industry and Macclesfield on her travels to various parts of the country. It was a much sought after role and the Silk Queen together with her Silk Princesses featured very prominently in the annual carnival and other parades enjoyed by the townspeople. Whole communities entered the carnival and the numerous parades, in fancy dress, on or accompanied by decorated floats with marching bands and dancers. Scouts, cubs and guides as well as the Mayor organised parades through the town with flags flying and bands playing. As a young lad I was always thrilled to march through the town as a member of the Christ Church Scouts with our flags fluttering in the breeze, the bugles blaring out and the kettle drums rhythmically throbbing while people stopped to watch us march by.

Although people lacked monetary wealth they had in those days a tremendous community spirit that in a way was wealth in itself. There was very little worth stealing and people trusted each other and indeed sharing was very much a street tradition. Very few neighbours were allowed to suffer unnecessarily. People banded together for their mutual enjoyment and church fetes, Sunday school functions, Rose Queen fetes and street parties would be organised with little financial requirement. Television did not plunder society and create inwardness and destroy neighbourliness. On summer days and nights people would flock to the parks and play bowls, picnic, play tennis or just listen to the many bands, brass and jazz, playing for free in the bandstands. Simple lives, simple pleasures and the family circle for many was still a warm, comforting environment unimpaired by the need for material goods and the pursuit of wealth. Football flourished as a cheap form of entertainment and most scouts, cubs, factories, churches and schools had their own team entered into a local league or just playing regular friendly matches. Cricket too, perhaps not as widespread but still it flourished on an ad hoc basis.

In 1937 the town enjoyed a national profile when Heath's were commissioned to make the silk gown for Elizabeth to be worn at the coronation of her husband King George VI.

Further social change was in the air as the new council housing policy commenced with purpose built dwellings for the people starting with the development of the Moss Estate.

However this period of stability and comparative prosperity was about to be destroyed when once again war clouds loomed over Europe and men were conscripted to fight the Germans, in the Second World War.

History repeated itself and once again it was the Macclesfield women who turned their skills to the war effort. Some factories were converted to enable munitions work to be carried out. The wiring of bombs for which the dextrous fingers of the skilled Macclesfield workforce were ideally suited was just one of several contributions to the war effort. Other mills turned their attention to the manufacture of silk parachutes, the quality of which was absolutely vital for the safety of the airmen so dependent on this last line of preservation. Many pilots and airmen owed their lives to the skill of Macclesfield operatives and some of the factories operated a 24 hour production system with Heath's mill turning out more than 800 parachutes a week!

The community spirit triumphed once again as Britain called for extra resources to assist in the war effort and there were regular fund raising campaigns to assist in specific theatres of the war. Many men were fighting overseas and families were left very much to fend for themselves but once again sharing and caring were the bye-words of the war effort and for many the burdens of food rationing, fuel shortages and sadly for some, the loss of a loved one was cushioned by the street and caring neighbours system. The town still enjoyed its parades and fetes, its cinemas and local dance halls, the Stanley Hall, Drill Hall, etc and some semblance of a normal life was perpetrated. However there were visitors in the form of evacuees seeking shelter from the more endangered bombing areas and exotic overseas visitors in the shape of Americans and Canadians. Local men answered the call for volunteers and some 500 men put themselves forward to form a Macclesfield Home Guard.

Mercifully Macclesfield escaped without any serious bombing incidents but there were three deaths after a bomber shed its load over Over Peover.

As the war officially came to an end the loss of life of Maxonians during the war years amounted to 195.

The boys came marching home once again to a world that had changed and could never be the same. Victory in Europe Day was an opportunity in 1945 for the people to let their hair down and rejoice that once again freedom had been maintained but sadly at a cost. The town celebrated with an enthusiastic patriotic joy, borne out of relief. Prime Minister Winston Churchill was rewarded for his wartime heroics by defeat in the 1945 General Election and a Labour government under Attlee took over to help recovery. Macclesfield elected a conservative to serve as its MP, Air Commodore Arthur Vere Harvey who would represent Macclesfield for 30 years and would be followed by Nicholas Winterton who would represent the town for another 30+ years.

Just after the war my family moved to the town from a war-ravaged Birkenhead and after several stays in various temporary lodgings we settled down for a few years in a rented terraced house with another resident living on the top floor at 108 Waters Green. I recall the very severe winter of 1946/7 and my father telling me of walking to Bollington in deep snow to work in a factory and of queuing for coke at the gas works at the foot of Hibel Road. He had managed to borrow a wheelbarrow or something similar from the farm of one of my uncles because you had to collect whatever you could in whatever you had. For my family and for nearly all families it was a time of austerity and deprivation. Heating came from an open fire provided you were lucky enough to have some kind of fuel to fire it. Severely cold weather resulted in windows frozen inside and out and bedtimes called for dressing up, not undressing. Old coats, blankets, socks – anything was utilised to keep out the cold weather in the cold, sparse, draughty Victorian bedroom and the bed I shared with my brother. Rationing of even the basics, like bread and butter resulted in massive queues. Ration coupons would be saved and built up for something just a little more special and huge queues formed, for example for cigarettes and sweets. Coal, fuel of any kind was scarce. Families like my own would gather round the wireless to listen to Palm Court, Dick Barton, and Journey Into Space, etc, for it was for most of us the only affordable form of entertainment.

In a grim period for the town there were in the 1940s a couple of bright spots. In 1947 the celebrated actor John Mills came to the town to shoot a film called *So Well Remembered* also starring Patricia Roc. Local people were used as extras and several recognisable locations were used in the film which caused a great deal of excitement. In 1949 an even greater honour was bestowed on a grateful township when the young Princess Elizabeth and husband, the Duke of Edinburgh arrived on 27th June, 1949 at Hibel Road railway station and were formally greeted and welcomed in the Market Place by Town Clerk, Walter Isaac. The soon to be Queen was presented with a length of jacquard woven silk as a gift together with silk handkerchiefs for Prince Charles during a visit to Brocklehurst Whiston Amalgamated (BWA) to commemorate her historic visit. Huge crowds lined the streets which were hung with flags and bunting and greetings messages. It was just the boost that a town worn down and jaded from the struggle to overcome the deprivation of the war years needed. Empire Day was also an opportunity to get out onto the streets and celebrate with friends and neighbours sharing whatever was to hand.

Slowly the town recovered, the silk mills were in operation, rationing was over and new housing was springing up. The Weston Estate was being built in the 1950s and my family like many others moved there to give us a bright new start in purpose built housing.

On 6th February 1952, King George V1 died and the town held a memorial service for him at a packed Parish Church on Friday, 15th February; Macclesfield, indeed the whole country was in mourning. It meant that the young Elizabeth who had visited Macclesfield only 30 months previously would accede to the throne.

However 1953 was a particularly memorable year and seemed to create buoyancy and lift the morale of a populace getting accustomed to change. The war in Korea ended, two men Hillary and Tensing became the first to climb Mount Everest, the highest mountain in the world, England defeated Australia to win the cricket Ashes and, on 2nd June, 1953, the 26 years old Elizabeth was crowned Queen Elizabeth II. The town still retained very warm memories of her Majesty's recent visit and the Coronation celebrations took on a warmth and an involvement it seemed from the whole town. Whole streets including main shopping thoroughfares were bedecked with flags, large and small, bunting of all types and anything that had a royal connotation. People came out onto the streets to share their joy and bask in mutual celebrations, streets held their own parties; joy was unconfined the post war gloom was lifting.

More change was in the air and pop music, records, record players and television were becoming more commonplace in the home. The more traditional crooners, Sinatra and Crosby, were now being challenged by a more aggressive form of music from a young Elvis Presley and Bill Haley and His Comets, which captured the imagination of the young and horrified parents with their explicit movements; so incredibly harmless by today's standards. Social change was in the air.

In Macclesfield the young were moving with the times but then so was industry. Macclesfield had for so long relied on the purity of its silk production but the industry was now being threatened by the creation of crepes, rayon, nylon, etc, which were man-made. Many of Macclesfield's remaining silk mills recognised the threat and many changed their production methods and moved away from pure silk to embrace the new fibres. In addition, new industries were coming to the town in the form of large pharmaceutical companies like ICI and Ciba Geigy; so much so, that a new business park was created, the Hurdsfield Industrial Estate. Although some criticism has been levelled at those factories that deserted pure silk production and also at the efforts to persuade the chemical giants to come to the area, the decisions were the saving of the town. The new processing of man made fibres would certainly have led to many redundancies of skilled silk workers. It was timely that those who were laid off or who could see that the 'writing was on the wall' were able to re-skill and move to the new jobs afforded by the Industrial Estate. It was probably the saving of Macclesfield as a prosperous town but the final nail in the silk industry's coffin.

The silk industry in Macclesfield was by now almost deceased apart from a couple of specialist firms whose high quality product was still in demand.

The 1960s was perhaps the most controversial period in Macclesfield's modern history.

It started so well with the whole of 1961 being devoted to the celebration of the 700th Anniversary of the granting of the 1261 Royal Charter to Macclesfield. Throughout the year a programme of events embraced a Jazz Festival at the Drill Hall with Ken Colyer and the Terry Lightfoot Bands, a Royal visit from HRH Princess Alexandra of Kent, Brass Band Concert in Victoria Park, BBC Invitation Concert at the Drill Hall, Charter Anniversary Day Civic Reception and Dinner at the Town Hall, a Swimming Gala headed by Diana Wilkinson, Mayor's Sunday Procession including Mayors of all the Cheshire Boroughs, Cheshire XI v All-England XI cricket match at Victoria Road, Charter Music Festival at the King's School and several flower shows and artistic exhibitions. However the real highlight came on the day nearest the anniversary, Saturday, 3rd June, 1961 with a Pageant of Macclesfield History. The massive procession commenced at Westminster Road at 3pm and traversed seventeen of the town's streets before coming to its final destination at South Park at 5pm.

The procession was led off by St George, Patron Saint of England followed by a naval detachment from HMS Teazer, the ship that had been adopted by Macclesfield following Warship Week during the Second World War. The 32 strong band of the 102 Transport Column of the Royal Army Service Corps followed closely behind followed by tableau after tableau representing significant moments in Macclesfield's history enacted by local people dressed to reflect the occasion. Twenty-two scenes were replicated and were followed by the Band of the 7th Battalion The Cheshire Regiment, more tableaux and then a pageant of transport down the ages including a Sedan Chair that had belonged to Mrs Charles Roe and a procession of local horses. The last tableau was that of the Charter Queen and her four Charter Princesses attended by two ladies. All the ladies had been chosen following a competition organised by the Macclesfield County Express.

The day was concluded with a huge concert which commenced in the South Park at 7.30pm with music by the Cheshire Regiment 7th Battalion Band, St Paul's Choral Union, The Band of 102 (Cheshire)

Transport Column (RASC), dancing by pupils of the Patterson School of Dancing and dancing to the music of the Royal Army Service Corps Band; the live performances finished at 11.30pm. It was a fantastic day enjoyed by virtually the whole town and a day that promised so much for the new decade.

It was of course the 'swinging sixties' with trendy fashions, pop music, new buildings a bright new world in which anything goes. In Macclesfield in the building sense it was a question of anything goes. It seems that the planners got rather carried away with their 'off with the old' and sadly some very poor decisions were made with regard to the destruction and demolition of old landmarks in the desire to build anew. The destruction of large swathes of the old town destroyed a lot of the character of the town shaped over hundreds of years. It was swept away in days by a builders 'swinging ball' in the concrete and glass era. Planners are supposed to have foresight and not lament with hindsight, which several have in regard to decisions taken at that time.

In 1967 more than twelve acres of Macclesfield around the Victoria Park area embracing more than 500 houses were flattened and the huge blocks of soulless flats erected in their place became a blot on the skyline. Centuries of neighbourliness, chatting in the backyard while hanging out washing, sharing water, sitting on a front doorstep of an evening talking to neighbours, tending small gardens and sharing information, children playing together within sight of the front door; a way of life, swept away within a matter of weeks replaced by a series of 'dovecotes'. People placed in compartments one on top of another and when the door closed they became trapped in a television-dominated world with little contact with neighbours. The initial social change was compounded by offering some of the accommodation to Manchester overspill, bringing in people who did not know the area and in many cases did not want to mix and socialise. Many people had misgivings about the entire project and over the years the flats became notorious for criminality. Thirty years later the flats were demolished and replaced by individual dwellings restoring some sense of community. The second major blunder was the removal of a large part of the centre of the town at the rear of Castle Street, the Stanley Street area that included the Stanley Hall. Once again rows of terraced houses were demolished and replaced by the concrete and glass of the Grosvenor Shopping Centre. Hindsight is a wonderful thing but if those streets had been renovated and restored creating a cobbled area with Victorian Street lamps and quaint Dickensian styled shops, what an attraction the area would have been. Instead the Grosvenor centre is modern, efficient and bland and the flat roofed buildings forming part of Castle Street are singularly unappealing.

There was a magnificent stone clad building at the bottom of Chestergate on the corner opposite the Town Hall that was in modern times the home of the Westminster Bank, that sadly was demolished and the present awful building housing the Natwest Bank is a monstrosity of a replacement. Other hideous buildings that somehow got past the planners include, the British Tele-communications building located on Hibel Road, an eyesore if ever there was one, and the police station on Brunswick Street is not a patch on the old one. Planning permission for Sovereign Court in King Edward Street must have been granted by Stevie Wonder, as was the truly lamentable Central Station, which resembles a large cigarette kiosk. It defies understanding that any body of reasonably intelligent people could rationally approve these buildings as being in the public interest. During the 1970s a degree of

top: *awful NatWest bank*
middle: *dreadful Police Station*
above: *lamentable Central Station*

sanity was restored driven by one man's vision. Rod Hackney objected to the proposed demolition of the area around Black Road arguing that restoration was a far better option. He negotiated grants and organised a residents self-help scheme that proved to be very successful, not only in saving the properties but creating a template for other schemes. High Street, for example, was later saved using his methods. Hackneys work attracted the attention of Prince Charles who came to Macclesfield to see for himself and Hackney, for a time, was referred to as the 'Royal Architect'.

Sadly Macclesfield lost other distinctive features once permanent to the town not always, I hasten to add, the fault of the planners. Lost to a fire in 1931 was the Opera House on Catherine Street, a fine building that once hosted a variety of shows was completely destroyed and today only a car park marks the spot. A very fine iron fountain that featured in many old photographs of the town was located on Park Green but was dismantled and the iron used for the war effort during the Second World War. Windmill Street, as the name implies, once featured a superb windmill built by Charles Roe; sadly that too was demolished during the war.

Fortunately there still remain in Macclesfield several old buildings of distinction apart from the churches and public buildings and mills not previously mentioned. Jordangate House formerly Pear Tree House the home of John Brocklehurst, now hosting Imperium Law, was built in 1728, Charles Roe House built in the

top: *superb former Post Office building (1920s) now Cheshire Building Society*
above: *Jordangate House*

18th century is in Chestergate, the Old Bank Building in King Edward Street, Park Green House and the old library and Gentleman's Club just off Sunderland Street, both date from around 1770.

However there are a number of much older places fortunately still surviving. At the top of the 108 Steps to the right in the little side street off Churchside there is a cottage dating from the 16th century, in Chestergate there are three cottages currently comprising the business premises of Cachet and The Cook Shop which date also from the 16th century. Opposite them is the Bate Hotel, arguably the oldest existing building in the town. In King Edward Street the Unitarian Chapel opened in 1690 is still active. A wall plaque states that it was a public place for the religious worship of 'their majestyes William and Mary'.

There is now a much greater awareness and recognition that our heritage must be preserved and I am sure that these old buildings will not be allowed to go the way of so many in the past. Saying that, old habits resurfaced when permission was granted for the erection of the truly awful Cyprotex building in Beech Lane.

Getting away from buildings, the world was changing and the

top: *Chestergate 16th century buildings*
above: *Unitarian Chapel (1690)*

proliferation of the motor-car created social and employment mobility. Work in the past revolved around the factory virtually on the doorstep and people walked to work. As the mills shut down people ventured further afield seeking employment and the car became king. Habits were changing and although we did not know it at the time the silk industry was dying, the corner shop was disappearing as supermarkets appeared, the wage packet was

awful Cyprotex Building, Beech Lane

replaced by faceless computer slips and in 1971 our money, the currency that had sustained us for hundreds of years was traumatically replaced; no more pounds, shillings and pence. The cinemas started to close perhaps as television took its toll, people preferring entertainment in the comfort of their own homes. The town also acquired a new Member of Parliament, another conservative, Nicholas Winterton who would serve us for the next 30 or more years. Macclesfield needed to re-invent itself and it did. At various times in its history it had produced copper, cotton and silk and now all three once staple industries had all but disappeared. Progress often means change and the town centre started to become congested with more and more traffic and the traditional market place was removed from the front of the Town Hall and in 1988 Chestergate was fully pedestrianised.

Macclesfield Town Football Club after many years of trying finally achieved Football League status in 1997 and proud Maxonians would hear the town mentioned on television or radio as the results were read out.

Nothing lasts forever and the giant Imperial Chemicals Company was swallowed up by Astrazeneca who fortunately retained its presence both in Macclesfield and Alderley Park ensuring the jobs of more than 3,000 people. The site on the Hurdsfield Estate embraces more than a 100 acres and is of course a major employer. Ciba Geigy, now renamed Ciba, has retained its presence but is today largely an administrative arm employing about 90 people.

The town is still engaged in the textile industry, but has diversified into high tech, some light engineering, paper and plastics.

However, statistics reveal that Maxonians are an entrepreneurial lot and a great many people had become self-employed creating a myriad of small businesses. In addition many professional people possibly attracted by the fact that the town was surrounded on all sides by beautiful countryside, had excellent schools and convenient access to road, rail and the airport at Ringway, elected to live in the area and travel to business in Stockport or Manchester or, in my case, to Derby and to Liverpool!

As the town celebrated the Millennium and looked forward to the 21st century it was featured on several occasions in national surveys linking its affluence and prosperity with the more affluent areas of the south east of the country.

In July 2002 the whole town came out onto the streets to welcome Queen Elizabeth II on her second visit to Macclesfield; it was her Jubilee year and she was visiting the King's School to help celebrate the quincentenary of its founding in 1502.

In 2003, a Macclesfield band, Silk Brass, won a National Championship but that was insufficient however to prevent the town being named in The Times survey in 2004 as the most uncultured town in the country. It seemed somewhat incongruous that a town so affluent as Macclesfield should be tarred with such a title. However the survey pointed out that the town did not have a single cinema or the benefit of a theatre. It does have a museum at West Park and a silk museum and a silk heritage centre but sadly remained bottom of the league. Nevertheless pride was restored when in December 2006 a survey conducted by Sport England revealed that Macclesfield's citizens ranked third in the country for exercise activities with a whopping 29.3% engaging in some form of regular physical exercise. Further confirmation of what a healthy lot we are came in August 2008 from the GMB Union who gave Macclesfield men an average life expectancy of 78.8 years and women 82.5, well above national and regional levels. (Compare that to 1854 an average of 27!) Further figures from the Central and Eastern Cheshire Primary Care Trust (CECPCT) confirmed that the level of physical exercise by Macclesfield residents was well above national and regional figures. It was suggested that living in, and surrounded by, so much excellent countryside that the quality of the air in the area combined with exercise and determination of the people was the elixir to a long life.

Unsurprisingly then, that a further survey carried out by the British Household Panel that was linked to the UK Census embracing approximately 10,000 people in 5,500 British households , released in September 2008, surmised that Macclesfield was ranked fifth in Britain in terms of being the happiest place in which to live.

Low unemployment is of course a factor and the town's enviable figures released in December 2007 showed that only 1.23 per cent per 1,865 of population were out of work and set the average gross weekly wage at £559.90 against the North West average of £432.70.

Over the centuries the town has undergone a metamorphosis progressing from a market town, copper producer, cotton and then of course silk, to today's healthy combination of diverse interests embracing high technology industries, pharmaceuticals, textiles and a whole range of entrepreneurial self-employed Maxonians. Nevertheless, the town is once again facing yet another challenge. The death of the corner-shop was a great loss to communities, often being the font of all knowledge, an exchange centre for gossip and news. Very often a kind hearted shop keeper would respond in difficult times to such requests as, "my mam says she won't get paid until Friday can she pay then?" or simply "can we pay next week?" and a tab would be run up. It helped many families to exist and survive. The supermarket put a stop to that and today out of town superstores are tempting local people away from the town centre. The centre of Macclesfield appears to be slowly and inexorably dying with empty spaces or boarded up shop fronts punctuating once thriving shopping streets; just one of the many casualties was Woolworth's, which after operating in the town since 1927 closed its doors in Chestergate for the last time in 2009. Handforth Dean and the Trafford Centre are pulling people away from the town with their promise of multiple-choice shopping, restaurants and entertainment facilities. Nevertheless the town has risen to the challenge of change several times in it's past and no doubt will do so again. There is a promise of a new shopping centre on the horizon and the ever-present promise of a new cinema! If any of us can live that long!

King's School

On 24th July, 2002 Her Majesty, Queen Elizabeth II visited Macclesfield as part of her Jubilee celebrations and during her visit unveiled a commemorative stone to celebrate the quincentenary of the founding of King's School.

For more than 500 years the school has enjoyed a reputation par excellence for the standard of education and the part many of its old boys have played in the military, social and cultural history of this country bears testimony to the consistency of those standards over the centuries. Even from those early days pupils travelled from all over Cheshire to attend the school and still do today.

In King's School, Macclesfield can boast that it has unquestionably one of the finest schools in the country and certainly rivals Manchester Grammar School as the best in the north of England.

In 1502, Christopher Columbus embarked on his fourth voyage to the New World and discovered St Lucia, Honduras and Costa Rica; Montezuma became King of the Aztecs; Henry Vll was King of England. Led by artists such as Michaelangelo and Leonardo da Vinci, Europe was about to embark on the Renaissance bringing with it a thirst for knowledge and culture also fuelled by the success of explorers such as Columbus and Vasco da Gama. Men of vision were looking to new horizons and seeking to expand man's knowledge and education.

Macclesfield too had its saviour, a man of vision and foresight who believed very much in the need to educate. Sir John Percyvale was born in the Macclesfield area but left to find his fortune. He prospered as a merchant and in 1450 joined the Merchant Taylors of London, becoming a Freeman of the City of London in 1458, and was knighted and appointed Lord Mayor of London in 1487. By now a wealthy man he married an equally wealthy lady and together with rich, powerful, friends they formed a formidable influential circle. Fortunately Sir John and his friends, amongst who was Sir Richard Sutton of Prestbury and Thomas Savage, the Archbishop of York, had a sense of responsibility and a desire to help educate the young. It was Sir Richard who helped found Brasenose College Oxford and Thomas Savage who sold the land to Sir John that would provide Macclesfield's first school. Sir John willed funds to be used exclusively to provide teachers for the education of Macclesfield children in a 'free gramer Scole'. Despite his wealth and fame Sir John remembered his roots and clearly had affection for his hometown.

In 1502, his money was used to establish Perceyvale's School in the Parish Church of St Michael and All Angels close by the Savage Chapel and William Bridges was appointed to be its first schoolmaster.

The early years were comparatively uneventful but very soon the King, Henry VIII, fashioned the English Reformation and set himself apart from the Pope following a dispute over his marital status, breaking away from the Church of Rome. The king declared himself the owner of all the Church of England's land and set about selling much of it, which resulted in the dissolution of many monasteries. It was this environment that lead to the closing of Perceyvale's School in 1547. However this early period would produce a pupil who would come to be renowned in British literature. Raufe Holynzed or Ralph Holinshed believed to have been born in Sutton, Macclesfield in 1520 wrote *The Chronicles of England, Scotland, and Ireland* that William Shakespeare would later use as the basis and source for 14 of his plays.

Holinshed was the first of very many local King's School pupils to make a name for himself on the national scene.

Henry VIII died in 1547 and was succeeded by his ten-year old son Edward V1 which led to a more settled period and in 1552 the school was re-founded. The Charter dated 26th April, 1552 gave the school its new title, The Free Grammar School of King Edward V1 in Macclesfield and declared that 'henceforth there may and shall be one grammar school in Macclesfield aforesaid'.

A great teacher John Brownsherd, born in 1540, taught at the King's School before moving to teach in Stratford-upon-Avon. It is widely believed that during his time in Stratford Brownsherd taught the young William Shakespeare, before returning to Macclesfield where he died in 1589. The King's School link with Shakespeare led to the speculation that Shakespeare himself might have at some point attended the school. Indeed the school established a research project in 2002 to investigate, but it yielded no positive results.

Over the ensuing years the school continued to develop and command respect in the area, particularly amongst the wealthier inhabitants.

However, the Civil War of the 1640s presented a considerable conflict of loyalties and emotions. In 1642 an old boy of the school, Sir Thomas Aston, who would in 1645 die of battle wounds, took

Macclesfield for the Royalists, but was himself later defeated by Parliamentarian, Colonel Mainwaring whose two sons attended the school. Mainwaring then repelled an attack by the Royalists this time led by Colonel Legh, a governor of the school! The battle for Macclesfield involved a King's School governor, an old boy and a parent!

The end of the Civil War resulted in the death of King Charles 1 who was beheaded on 27th January, 1649. It was an old boy of King's, Judge John Bradshaw, who uniquely and notoriously signed the King's death warrant. Born in Stockport, Bradshaw became an attorney in Congleton where he later became mayor, before holding a series of powerful positions culminating in the appointment to England's Lord President of the Court, the presiding judge of England's highest court. Bradshaw continued to prosper becoming one of the country's wealthiest and most powerful citizens. After his death Charles II came to the throne and in an act of vengeance had Bradshaw's remains disinterred and hung them on the gallows at Tyburn. His head was later displayed at Westminster and his lands and wealth confiscated.

Around 1748, King's School was starting to outgrow itself and relocated to King Edward Street, where it continued to attract the offspring of Cheshire's wealthiest families.

In 1802, the school had 19-day pupils and 72 boarders, sleeping several to a bed, which demonstrates the fact that the pupils came from out of the immediate area. There is also evidence that in 1807 there existed an old boys club.

The school continued to expand and, following a desire to pursue a more modern system of education, land was purchased in 1838 in the Great King Street/Bridge Street area. In 1844 the Modern Schools building was completed, leaving the Grammar School at King Edward Street as the 'senior' school. By this time Macclesfield was starting to prosper and benefit from its development of the silk industry and there were more than 20 private schools serving the town as well as church schools for the poor.

The 1851 census revealed a town population of about 39,000 being serviced by 122 inns and 42 pubs! The area was attracting workers for the mills and businesses moved in on the back of full employment. According to one survey there were around 800 shops, several mills, coachbuilders and builders as well as the professions, surgeons and lawyers. A growing diverse population brought with it children who needed educating and the Grammar School found the need to expand and the decision was taken to move from King Edward Street.

King's School main building, viewed across the cricket pitch from Cumberland Street

A tract of open land, virtual countryside, was purchased in the area now located at Cumberland Street/ Westminster Road close by the old infirmary, now Sainsbury's, and the new complex was opened in 1855. During this time the school was in two parts, one consisting of The Grammar with 53 day boys and 13 boarders and the other Modern Schools, with 112 day pupils The Grammar was said to be the only school in Cheshire classed as a First Grade Grammar School. However, in 1910 the Grammar and Modern were amalgamated, embracing 200 pupils, and once again expansion was required and new building was undertaken on site and completed in 1912.

However, war clouds were gathering over Europe and the school paid a stiff price with the loss of 70 pupils killed in the First World War. Recovery was rapid and by the mid 1920s the school comprised 350 pupils with an annual Cheshire County scholarship of 25 boys.

In 1933 a 32-year old destined to become a King's School legend, Thomas Taylor Shaw, took over the role as Headmaster, a position he would hold for 33 years and also during my own time as a pupil.

Once again, war created havoc across the nation and 40 old boys paid the ultimate price for their country during the Second World War. During this time, in 1944, the school elected to become independent and Cheshire County Council agreed to buy places for boys passing the Eleven Plus exam. In 1956 I was one of the boys who benefited from such a scheme. I was at Parkroyal Secondary Modern School and was given the chance at Fourteen Plus to transfer to King's School, an offer that I grabbed with both hands.

Once again expansion was required to cope with over 1,000 pupils and a new building was added to the existing ones. I witnessed the opening ceremony conducted by the Duchess of Kent in 1957 when she inaugurated the new art block, The Kent Block.

Other milestones were the retirement of TT Shaw in 1966, the Government Assisted Places Scheme to help those who could not afford the full fees in 1981 and the groundbreaking decision to admit girls into the Sixth Form in 1986. In 1987 the decision was taken to make the junior division co-educational and after the purchase of Macclesfield High School For Girls in 1993 a Girl's Division for the age groups 11-16 was established. King's School has modernised and adjusted with the times and now affords education from the age of 3 until 18 for both male and female.

King's School continues to stress the importance of cultural and sporting activities to complement the desire for education. The balance to the pupil of healthy activity on the sports field invariably helps to combat the intensiveness of study. The benefit to the country from old boys prowess on the sports field and in the political, military, social and cultural fields has remained undimmed over the past 500 years and long may it continue to do so.

General Sir Ralph Abercromby sent his three sons to the school but it was the youngest, James, who was to become festooned with this country's highest honours.

He was, variously, Member of Parliament for Edinburgh, Judge Advocate General, and Master of The Mint, Lord Dunfermline, and Cabinet Minister to Prime Minister Lord Aberdeen in 1854 and in 1855 he was appointed Speaker of the House of Commons.

Former pupil James Parke later became Lord Wensleydale and George Long, in 1811, was a co-founder of the Royal Geographical Society. After the 1832 Reform Bill Macclesfield was able to elect a member for Parliament and two old boys were amongst the first to represent the town, John Ryle, Tory and John Brocklehurst, Liberal.

John Fielden Brocklehurst, later Lord Lieutenant of Rutland, had the rare distinction of being involved in two of Britain's historic military incidents. He was part of the British relief force that arrived too late to save General Gordon from being massacred at Khartoum in 1885 but during the Boer War (1899-1900) he took part in the great and successful defence of Ladysmith.

Another old boy, who left King's School in 1893, Hewlett Johnson achieved high prominence as the Dean of Canterbury before becoming notorious for his sympathies with Marxism which earned him, in 1951, the unique accolade from the Soviet Union of the Stalin Peace Prize. His views were however regarded as treasonable by much of the British public.

A number of old boys have had their skills and contributions to Britain's well being recognised through knighthoods and awards of Commander of the (Order of the) British Empire, Officer of the (Order of the) British Empire and Member of the (Order of the) British Empire. Sir Clive Booth, who left King's in 1962, became Chairman of the Central Police Training and Development Authority and Professor Sir Edward Anthony Wrigley, in 1996, became Master of Corpus Christi College and wrote many books and papers on wealth and population.

The CBE was granted in 2003 to Crispian Strachan, the Chief Constable of Northumbria who left King's in 1967, to D.A. Porter who left in 1972, to Ken Culley, who was a classmate of mine in the late 1950s, in 1998 (more of KC later in the book) and to Peter Ellwood in 2001.

Peter Ellwood attended King's School from 1954-1961, during my time at the school, and although I do not recall meeting him then we were to meet later in our professional capacities. Peter eventually, before retiring, in 1997 became Chief Executive of Lloyds TSB Group plc, which at the time was the largest bank in Great Britain (more of him in a later chapter).

OBE's have been awarded to Captain J.R. Turner who left school in 1945, to Professor Peter Downes, Chair of the British Biochemical Society for his services to medical research, to Neil Makin, who left in 1965, for his services to Adult Learning in 2005 and to an old cricketing colleague of mine Norman H Walker, who left in 1958. The MBE was awarded in 2008 to Macclesfield's Keith Yearsley, who left King's School in 1951.

Other old boys who earned great distinction in service to this country in the diplomatic service and politics are Tony Golds, who left sometime in the 1930s and was Ambassador to the Republic of Cameroon, Gabon and Equatorial Guinea from 1970-72, and from 1972-74 was High Commissioner to Bangladesh, and Alan Beith, from

Poynton, who became MP for Berwick upon Tweed. He was at King's School from 1954 to 1961 and was indeed a classmate of mine. For a time he was the sub editor of the Poynton Post but after going to Oxford University and becoming, for a short time, a lecturer at Newcastle University he entered politics. He was elected MP for Berwick upon Tweed in 1973 and has held the post ever since. From 1985-87 he was the Liberal spokesman on Foreign Affairs and Chief Whip from 1976-87. In 1992 he was appointed Chief Whip of the newly formed Liberal Democrat Party and later was elected as Deputy Leader of the Liberal Democrat Party.

John Blundell, who left King's School in 1971, is the Director General of the Institute of Economic Affairs, a much respected and, many say, the leading think tank in the world. Someone else who has received the ultimate accolade in his profession is Captain Ken Owen, who left King's in 1951, and who in 2004 was nominated Shipmaster of the Year, the highest award that the Nautical Institute can award to a member.

In the field of sport King's School has always commanded respect in many of the sporting disciplines, especially cricket and rugby, and has won very many county, regional and national competitions. A great many old boys have, for example, represented Cheshire over the years in a whole range of sports but this book is dealing specifically with national recognition.

Uniquely, in the 1908 Olympic Games, Gerald Mason captained the Great Britain lacrosse team, which also included old boy Johnson Parker Smith. Nearly 100 years later, Ben McAllister (1995) kept goal for England in the World Lacrosse Championships in Perth in 2002 and kept goal again in the European Championships in Prague in 2005. In 1909, F. G. Handforth from Prestbury, represented England at rugby earning four international caps and going on to play for the British Lions in 1910 and later the Barbarians.

However, King's Schools greatest rugby player is without question England international and British Lions and Barbarians regular Steve Smith who was at the school from 1962-68, more of him in the chapter on sportsmen.

Cricket has always been a great tradition at the school and in 2007 King's School commemorated 150 years of cricket on the front field of Cumberland Street. For many of us that front field was our own 'field of dreams'. I enjoyed playing for the first eleven and actually had the distinction of hitting a six over the wall into Cumberland

Street to win a match against Cotton Grammar School in 1957 or 58. I was duly admonished for my 'Kevin Pietersen' moment by cricket master and umpire 'Dickie' Edwards. Although my team-mates were suitably excited by the blow, 'Dickie' put me down with "nice hit Burrows but we were 7 wickets down at the time and that ball was bang on your middle stump. If you had missed it we might have lost the game".

The school has regularly supplied Cheshire with county players and several went on to play with other counties. The late Mike Davis, an old friend and contemporary, had a particularly promising cricket career sadly cut short by injury. However two old boys Freddie Millett and Peter Moores both made an impact on the national scene and are featured individually in later chapters.

King's School had the privilege of adding to its former pupils honour board a Yachting Champion. Robert Cooper, who left school in 1986 and won the 2005 Sigma Class in the European Championships,

A most unique and proud achievement which proves that the modern day King's School pupils are every bit as good as their illustrious predecessors was announced in 2004. Oliver Burr, who left King's School in 2000, and who had at the age of 13 become the youngest person ever to climb the Matterhorn, became in May 2004 the youngest person ever to climb Everest: a most remarkable achievement and a classic example of the old adage upwards and onwards.

However, the tradition at the school has been to concentrate on the all round development of students believing that competitive sport is an ideal counter balance to academic learning while, at the same time, trying to create and nurture interest in cultural and musical activities. Success was amply demonstrated when the 100 strong King's School choir in 2003 was voted in a nationwide competition as the Songs of Praise Senior School Choir of The Year.

The future is clearly in good hands, especially with the news in 2008 of King's Girls' Division student Jennifer Pinches recognition as one of the country's brightest prospects in the gymnastics field. Jennifer is the Junior English and British Schools All Round champion and is currently ranked eighth in Europe. Her potential is such that she was invited to Beijing for the 2008 Olympics as an observer, to help promising athletes like herself to become acclimatised to the Olympic atmosphere, in anticipation of the 2012 Olympics in London.

It appears that Great Britain has potentially another Ben Ainslie on its hands (the triple Olympic gold medal yachtsman) in the guise of King's School's 14-year-old Elliot Hanson. To date Elliot has exceeded Ben's achievements at British junior level by winning junior sailing championships, the World Title, National Championship, the Inland Championship and the Nationwide Series, Gul Topper class. No one has ever attained this level of dominance until Elliot's amazing emergence. He promises to emulate the wonderful achievements of Ainslie, a fellow Maxonian. To help realise his undoubted potential he has been recommended for a Sports Aid grant to assist in training ahead of the 2012 Olympics.

Colleagues, readers and knowledgeable Maxonians will note that there are a number of very familiar names missing from this chapter, all old boys of King's School.

Ian Curtis and Steven Morris of Joy Division, opera singer Peter Forbes Robinson, England cricket coach Peter Moores, Michael Jackson, former controller of BBC television, Geoff Lloyd, Radio presenter and cricketer Freddie Millett MBE. The reason that they are omitted from this sector is because they were all born or brought up in Macclesfield and their lives are featured individually in later chapters.

Sporting Heroes

Olympians

Track Cycling – Reg Harris OBE

In 2008 Britain's cyclists dominated the World Championships and later that year won eight gold medals at the Beijing Olympics. Our cycling team has established new standards and the sport, centred nationally on the magnificent Manchester Velodrome, has grown enormously in popularity. However, while we quite rightly enjoy the euphoria of such dominance, we need reminding that once before, through the supreme talent of one individual track cyclist for a time, a golden time, Britain enjoyed similar supremacy.

Reginald Harris was born in Bury in March 1920 but started his connection with Macclesfield after serving in the Second World War

Harris statue in Manchester Velodrome

in Africa. Following the collapse of his first marriage in 1947 he met Macclesfield girl, Dorothy Hadfield, later that year and after a dinner date and a deepening relationship with her he came to know Macclesfield well. He was already making a name for himself in the world of track cycling and, as the World Amateur Champion in 1947, was the hot favourite to win Olympic Gold at the games to be held in London in 1948.

Sadly it was not to be; just before the games he suffered a broken arm and was not expected to be fit enough to compete. It was a testimony to his drive and sheer determination that not only did he make the Games but won a silver medal in the individual sprint and a silver in the tandem event. Many athletes under the circumstances would have regarded such an achievement as a success but to Reg it was failure. He turned his back on the amateur sport and turned professional in 1949.

In the meantime he married Dorothy and they came to live with her parents in Macclesfield whilst looking for somewhere to live on a permanent basis. For a time he trained in the local lanes surrounding the town and the long strait from Macclesfield to Chelford was an ideal road for cyclists to indulge in a prolonged sprint.

For the next five years or so, Reg Harris was the undisputed leading racing cyclist in the World, winning the World Professional Championship in 1949, 1950, 1951 and 1954, breaking the world kilometre record five times. In addition he was voted Britain's Sportsman of the Year on two occasions and was awarded the OBE for his services, not only to cycling but also to British sport.

However, in 1956 he finished runner-up in the World Championship and characteristically regarded this as failure and retired from the sport.

For a time he served as manager of the Fallowfield Stadium, later re-named the Harris Stadium, but then decided to go into the cycling manufacturing business with a close friend who had experience in light engineering. Harris returned to Macclesfield and opened his factory. Sadly his second foray into the town was much less successful than his first. He recalled in his book, *Two Wheels To The Top*, "The cost of finding these experts (people skilled in constructing cycles) and helping them move to Macclesfield was the first nail in my financial coffin".

After three years the business folded along with Harris's second marriage to Dorothy, broken by the stress and strain of the faltering business, and he went to Lancashire to work with Gannex. After a short spell there he returned to Macclesfield once again when taking up a post with Kay Brothers Plastics, based in Bollington. (Authors note. My wife also worked at Kay's during this time, as did a nearby neighbour of ours Jennifer Anne Geary.)

Harris married Jennifer Geary in 1970, after divorcing Dorothy, and shortly afterwards decided on a return to the race track and, unbelievably, in 1974 at the age of 54, won the British Sprint Championship proving that old truism that 'form is temporary, class is permanent'. It was a brief re-union with his sport and typically once he had proved that he could 'do it' he was happy to let the achievement speak for itself.

For Reg his last marriage was a happy one and he and Jennifer were still together in 1992 when he had a stroke whilst cycling in his beloved Cheshire countryside and died.

Reg Harris OBE is buried in the grounds of Chelford church, a place he must have cycled past many times on his training or social rides and his headstone lists his many considerable achievements.

In addition there is a superb statue of him in the Manchester Velodrome that I am certain must have helped inspire our present crop of world-beaters to their present day eminence.

This much-garlanded Maxonian was the standard bearer for a later generation benefiting from technological advances in the sport but still acutely aware of the standard he set.

Headstone, Chelford Church

Swimmer – Steve Mellor
Since the founding of the Macclesfield Amateur Swimming Club in 1893, the town has produced several excellent swimmers who having

learned their skills at Davenport Street baths went on to achieve commendable results at national level.

Fred Bramhall became a National England Champion in 1930 and for several years featured on the national scene. I can recall the tall Betty Blackburn who for nine years dominated swimming in the north of the country, winning the Northern Counties Backstroke title nine times! Brenda Sherratt achieved national fame and renown when in 1966 she became the first person to swim Loch Ness.

However, someone personally known to me who was also a school-friend of my wife, Valerie Brown, not only became the English Schools Backstroke Champion but also in 1962 became an international trialist just failing to make the British Olympic team and the Commonwealth Games team. Valerie however would achieve a degree of vicarious success when her youngest son, Steven Mellor, became an Olympian at the age of 19 when selected to represent Great Britain at the Olympic Games in Barcelona 1992.

Born in Macclesfield on 11th March, 1973, Steve was taught to swim by his mother from the age of 3. The family, father John and older brother Simon, lived at Benbrook Way, Gawsworth and sport was very much to the fore in the Mellor household. Valerie was very active at the Macclesfield Swimming Club and later the Macclesfield Satellite Club, the more competitive side of the organisation. Simon and Steve were both good swimmers and father John was into rugby. Both boys attended Broken Cross School and, at the age of eight, Steve was swimming with the Satellite Swimming Club and won his first competitive race in the prestigious Stockport Shrimps event. At the age of 10 he competed in the National Championships for under 11's at Blackpool and at the age of 12 was a National Champion. He was now at Henbury High School and junior England honours quickly followed before winning his first swimming cap for England at the age of 18. He was making a name for himself and one or two American universities came in with scholarship offers but Steve believed that his future would best be served by remaining at home, preferring stability as the challenges grew.

Davenport Street baths had now been closed and replaced by the Macclesfield Leisure Centre and Steve was grateful for their support in the generous supply of training opportunities.

Although he was performing well, there was still the little matter of the Olympic trials at Sheffield after which the Olympic team would be selected. He performed superbly at the trials breaking his personal

Steve Mellor (courtesy of Chapter 1 Sports)

best times in all his events and was very unlucky to miss out on selection for the individual events, particularly the 400 metres freestyle when he finished third. Although only the first two could be selected his time put him in the top 20 in the world! Nevertheless he was selected for the 4 x 200 relay quartet and told the local press " I don't think it has really sunk in yet".

By the time the team left for the Olympic Training Camp in the South of France, Great Britain's relay quartet were ranked sixth in the world and would therefore have an excellent chance of reaching the final and perhaps a medal. Sadly it was not to be; reach the final they did but finished sixth. To reach any Olympic final is an achievement in itself and for always to be regarded as an Olympian, the highest accolade an athlete can attain, is an honour forever cherished.

In 1994 Steve became Great Britain National Senior Champion, USA National Champion and a Commonwealth Games Medallist. For a number of years he continued to compete and travelled around the world competing in masters events with some success. In 2001 he became the World Masters Record Holder and European Masters Champion.

Older brother Simon Mellor, no mean athlete himself, went on to win a National Triathlon title, swimming, running and shooting with another Macclesfield lad, a former neighbour of mine, David Cooper. Today Steve Mellor lives in Woodford and runs a successful business utilising his knowledge of sport, training facilities and travel requirements for sports organisations across the board. His company Sports Abroad only started in 2006 and is now starting to show the benefits of his experiences. Rugby clubs – most recently London Irish became a client – are a target market and Sports Abroad are currently talking to a number of Premier League Football clubs anxious to take advantage of professional travel/training expertise.

As a swimmer Steve Mellor attained a very high level of performance, stayed true to his roots and honoured the loyalty of his many supporters. He is the first modern, homegrown Maxonian to be called an Olympian and that is in itself a unique honour.

Hockey – Sean Kerly MBE
Although not Macclesfield born, Sean Kerly became the first Maxonian who spent his formative years in the town to become not only an Olympian but also a medal winner.

Born in Whitstable, Kent on 29th January, 1960 Sean was a toddler when he came to Macclesfield with his family.

In his later years, when he became a favourite with the media, he told of his great love for Macclesfield and his early memories. He told of playing football as a cub scout in the town and recalled with horror his first frightening experience of heading a wet, heavy leather soccer ball. The old leather balls weighed a ton especially when wet and only the brave hearted would dare head a ball in flight. Perhaps it was that which helped turn Sean to his great love hockey. He went to Ivy Bank School where some years later my own children would attend and enjoyed playing football. His great success in hockey he, in part, attributed to the help and advice given him by the Ivy Bank games master, Alan Capper. Sean said that it was Alan who had taught him about football tactics, which later on in his life he so successfully adapted, to hockey.

His family left Macclesfield and returned to Kent and Sean completed his education at Chatham House Grammar School, Ramsgate where he played rugby and started his interest in hockey. Very soon he started to acquire a reputation as a tough no nonsense attacking forward with a penchant for aggression and scoring goals in the local league. England recognised his dash and tenacity and international call up became inevitable. Great Britain qualified for the Olympic games in Los Angeles and it was Sean's proudest moment of his career when he was selected for the team and became an Olympian. The team did well and finished with a bronze medal. However, away from the glamour and the spotlight Sean, unlike many of his international opponents, had to work and he had during his career a variety of jobs. It was he admitted hard to embark on a structured career when time had to be allocated to training and often, prior to big events, having to go away for weeks on end. Jobs became dispensable; in his time he has been a trainee accountant, a jewellery chain merchandising manager, transport manager and several other make do occupations.

The next great challenge, in terms of hockey, came with the World Cup tournament in 1986 where Britain beaten by Australia, won the silver medal and yet again, in 1987 during the European Championships, Britain got another silver. It seemed that the ultimate title of champions was evading a very good Great Britain side, in which Kerly was becoming renowned for his 'Bobby Charlton' scoring prowess.

Kerly was selected for the Great Britain team for the 1988 Olympics in Seoul, South Korea and he remembers that the team were all highly conscious of their 'nearly' status and mindful of the bronze four years earlier in 1984.

In the semi final they met old rivals Australia and in a very tough match they triumphed 3-2 with Sean Kerly scoring a fantastic hat trick. In the final they met West Germany and at last became Olympic gold medal winners beating the Germans 3-1 with Kerly netting yet again.

The team returned home heroes, won the BBC Sports Personality of The Year Team Award and Sean Kerly was actually nominated in the individual capacity and became somewhat of a cult figure. Chat shows, radio and television, pantomime, interviews, meetings at Buckingham Palace with the Queen and at No 10 with Prime Minister Margaret Thatcher; it was all very heady stuff and yet as Sean remembers he came home a hero but had no job to go to.

He later admitted that he did not make the most of his spot in the limelight in terms of commercial promotion but continued with the hockey and was selected for the 1992 Olympic games in Barcelona. Incidentally, Macclesfield's Steve Mellor remembers meeting Sean in Barcelona during the Olympics. Great Britain finished sixth and for Sean it was the end of his international career although he continued to play for Canterbury.

Over eleven years representing his country, his international career embraced 198 caps for Great Britain and England in which he scored an amazing 100 goals. His tremendous record was recognised when he was awarded the Medal of the British Empire (MBE) in 1993 for his service to British hockey. Further honours came his way when he was appointed Chairman of the Athletes Panel of the International Hockey Federation in 2003.

Sean still has a very active interest in hockey and has been to all the recent Olympics and major tournaments as a media commentator. He is very active in the Canterbury area and is trying to raise national awareness of hockey, as he believes that it needs wider and more complete exposure. He is still very passionate about the game and, although today he is a keen golfer, he still turns out for the lower Canterbury hockey teams when able.

He presently lives in Herne Bay with his partner and their three teenage daughters, two of whom play hockey, and Sean works as a marketing consultant.

Sean Kerly is undoubtedly Britain's best known player, if not best ever hockey player, and his records may never be beaten. It is gratifying to know that those very early seeds of tenacity and ambition were sown on the small playing field of Ivy Bank School, Macclesfield and eventually yielded Olympic Gold.

Sailing – Ben Ainslie CBE OBE

A man swiftly becoming not only Macclesfield's most famous Olympian but also threatening to become as successful as the great Sir Steve Redgrave, is Macclesfield born Ben Ainslie. Ben now has the phenomenal record of three Olympic gold and one Olympic silver medal and has been described in the media as Britain's most famous sailor since Nelson; praise indeed. In terms of Olympic performance he is now officially Britain's foremost sailor since beating the two gold medals and silver won by the legendary sailor Rodney Pattison who was dominant in the 1960s and 70s.

Born in the town on 5th February, 1977, Ben attended the Terra Nova School close to Jodrell Bank. Mum, Sue Ainslie who was born in Adlington, told the Macclesfield Express that although Ben had enjoyed growing up in the Macclesfield area they had decided to move away to live closer to the sea. Toddler Ben started sailing or taking an interest in sailing at the age of three or four, hardly surprising, as father Rodney had taken part in the first Whitbread Round The World Race in 1973, and having built the vessel with brother-in-law Ian Butterworth, they finished an amazing fourth out of seventeen competitors. Ben's early experience was sailing on Redesmere Lake supplemented by weekend trips to North Wales starting to learn the rudiments. Clearly there was an element of persuasion and an influence from the family gene pool! He told a national newspaper that his first memorable sailing experience and his best ever holiday was when he was seven and spent a holiday sailing around the Greek Islands with his parents. He recalled helping to sail the boat, doing jobs on board, fishing and windsurfing. It really gave him the taste for what was to come.

At the age of eight the family removed to Cornwall and Ben took part in his first competition at Restronguet Creek, Cornwall in 1985 and in 1988 won the national under 12 title.

He was a quick learner and his qualities of patience and determination were very evident when he won the World Youth Championship in 1995 and, at the age of 19, in 1996 he was selected for the 1996 Atlanta Olympics in the Laser Class.

One would think that a silver medal in your first Olympics would be reward indeed but not for Ben Ainslie. During the decisive race in the Laser class, the gold was between Ainslie and Robert Scheidt and many observers believed that Scheidt employed aggressive tactics bordering on the unsportsmanlike, to upset the young Briton and win the gold. Ainslie, although bitterly disappointed, remembered this lesson and four years later during the Sydney Olympics Ben did exactly the same to Scheidt to win the gold. A close friend once described Ainslie as the most competitive man in the world. Competitive, tough, determined and resilient – all the qualities required in a top sportsman.

Since partaking in his first Olympics in 1996 Ben has since then won seven world championships. Indeed the only year he failed to win a title was in 2007 when he did not actually compete, as he was helmsman in the Emirates Team New Zealand boat that failed to wrest the title from the Swiss holder, Team Alinghi. Although he is not used to losing Ben agreed that it had been a fantastic experience and he was hoping to carry that forward to the next Americas Cup in which he will compete in the Team Origin, Britain's new challenger. Compete he will, both as helmsman and skipper, an honour indeed.

It is often forgotten that many of our Olympic athletes are essentially amateurs, although some do get lottery funding, and in between competing many of them have to make a living. Sailors do it by becoming crew members for large boats or try through reputation to become attached to the America's Cup squads.

After winning gold in Sydney, Ainslie decided that he needed a new challenge and he won the right to represent Britain in Athens in 2004 but this time competing in the heavier Finn class. The challenge was met and he became an Olympic gold medallist for the second time. He continued winning international events and, despite little competitive racing, won the right to go to Beijing in 2008, again in the Finn class. After winning his third gold Ben told the world press that the ever-changing conditions in Beijing were amongst the hardest that he had experienced and that he had been tested to the limit. His skill and determination were acknowledged by his closest rival with whom he had had a robust contest when the American, Zach Railey said at the end of the competition "Ben is the best dinghy sailor the world has ever seen" – generous praise from a competitive rival.

One would think that such a skilled and accomplished sailor made very few errors or indeed would admit to making errors. However, he did comment on one incident. On one occasion he was sailing a Laser 500 with good friend and Olympic gold medal sailor Iain Percy. In mitigation he claimed that the boat was new to both of them, nevertheless these accomplished international sailors somehow wrecked and beached the boat on a sand bar off Hayling Island and were ignominiously rescued by the RNLI Inshore Lifeboat; most embarrassing for world class sailors.

Ben doesn't get too much spare time but when he does he plays golf, likes watching movies and reading and supports Chelsea FC, if only from an armchair.

The question everyone is asking is will he be back for a fifth Olympic games in 2012 on home ground, or rather home waters, in London. Ben is aware just how wonderful it would be to win gold at home but it is two years away and much can happen in that time. At the moment he is non- committal as he would be 35 at the time of the next games.

Now the Olympics are over he is very much focussed on the America's Cup and is determined to bring the trophy back to Britain. Who would bet against him?

In the meantime his hometown Macclesfield is discussing just what sort of honour they can bestow on the town's most famous Olympian. A number of councillors have proposed that he be given the freedom of the town and the matter is to be discussed in detail at a future gathering. It is a matter of great pride when one of our fellow citizens achieves fame across the world and the name of our small town comes to the fore.

In September 2008, Ben was interviewed by the Macclesfield Express and joked that if he were made a Freeman of the Borough "could that get me free pints in the Macc pubs?"

In December he came fourth in the BBC's Sports Personality of the Year award and was awarded the CBE in the Queen's New Years honours list.

Although he now lives in Lymington and his late grandparents used to live in Knutsford and Wilmslow, he still comes back to this area to visit an uncle.

"I had a great time growing up in Macclesfield and used to sail at Redesmere" he said and then he added, somewhat modestly, "It's good to know the people of Macclesfield remember me". Ben Ainslie,

OBE, Olympic Champion – how can we possibly not know the most famous British sailor since Horatio Nelson.

Cricket

Freddie Millett, MBE

Macclesfield has for many years had a great tradition of supplying quality cricketers both from the Macclesfield Club and particularly from the King's School. In almost conveyor like numbers, Cheshire, in particular, has benefited. I know from my own time of playing in the local leagues and playing at King's School, numerous players went on to represent the county and some went to play for other counties in the County Championships. I played with and against Richard Cragg, Alan McInnes, Clive Barker, John Higginson, Brian Lowe, Mike James and Mike Davis, who all played for Cheshire after leaving King's School. Mike Davis went on to play for Northants, Peter Moores went to Middlesex, before moving even higher up the cricket ladder and Macclesfield born Jonathan Agnew played for Leicestershire and England. Since my time of course there has been many more.

For very many years, however, Macclesfield and Cheshire cricket was carried it seemed on the shoulders of Frederick W Millett or Freddie, as he was universally

Freddie Millett, MBE

known. He was a massive presence on the cricket scene and went on to have a national profile.

He was born in Macclesfield on 30th March, 1928 and lived at 79, Commercial Road. His mother was Florence Biddulph and his father Frederick was a slipper and shoemaker. Freddie was educated at King's School before moving on to Leicester Technical College and then spent some time in the air force. He was playing cricket at this time with Leicestershire and then moved back to Macclesfield to work at Castle Shoe Company just off Waters Green. A hard-hitting batsman who could bat anywhere in the order – opener or number 6 he was equally versatile. He could also bowl at a lively medium pace and became a permanent fixture in the Macclesfield team, indeed captaining the side for more than fourteen years. He was a tough uncompromising captain who did not take kindly to defeat. These qualities stood him in great stead when captaining Cheshire from 1960-70s in the Minor Counties championships and actually winning the national title in 1967. Such was his quality, as a player that while captaining the Minor Counties at the age of 41 against the touring, all conquering West Indies side of 1969, he scored 102 not out. He represented the English Minor Counties League on seven occasions. Freddie would happily have spent his life just playing cricket but after his father died in 1964 he had a business to run and Freddie Millet & Co, based at Queens Avenue, demanded his attention away from the cricket field.

I have the distinction of claiming Freddie Millett's wicket on a memorable afternoon in 1958 when playing for the King's School in the annual match against Macclesfield Cricket Club. I had bowled against him without success but when I was fielding he hit a powerful shot straight at me at mid-off. The newspaper reported, "Millett was splendidly caught by Burrows". What the paper did not report was the fact that I had little choice; the shot was drilled so hard at me that I had to jack-knife to avoid being cut in two! Although it was a good catch Freddie was not too enthused at being dismissed; typical of his competitiveness.

He received the MBE for his services to cricket in 1979 and spent more than fifteen years serving on the Marylebone Cricket Club (MCC) committee. Another highlight of his career was being appointed manager of the MCC Touring side to America in 1982. When he died in 1991 at the age of 63, he was chairman of the Minor Counties selection committee – still serving the game he had loved for more than 40 years.

It was on a trip to London in January 1963 that he met a young lady, Diane, and they were married just weeks later in May 1963. Diane still lives in the Macclesfield area and has served as a Macclesfield Borough Councillor and as a representative governor on the King's School Governing Body.

Freddie Millett was a giant in Cheshire cricket and was the first to make an impact on the national scene.

Jonathan Agnew
BBC Cricket Correspondent – Head of Test Match Special
Jonathan Agnew was born in Macclesfield on 4th April, 1960 to Philip and Margaret Agnew. His family were farmers from Dukenfield Hall Farm, Mobberley but during his early years the family moved to Leicestershire, where Jonathan was educated at Uppingham School.

It was here that he developed his love for cricket. Tall and thin he found that he was able to propel the ball at speed and became as a junior, a formidable right arm fast bowler in the local leagues before playing for the Surrey Second team in 1977 and then the Leicestershire Second XI. He really came to prominence when, after making his debut for the Leicestershire first team early in 1978 and taking a wicket with only his fourth ball, he later that year was selected for the MCC Schools team, the National Cricket Association Young Cricketers and England Young Cricketers.

During his relatively short but successful playing career, which officially ended in 1990 and embraced 12 years, 'Aggers' as he is universally known in the quaint language attributed to cricket, took 666 wickets at an average of 29.25; highly respectable with a career best of 9-70 against Kent in 1985. Although he was no great shakes as a batsman he did make a career best score of 90 against Yorkshire in 1987.

However, in 1984 he became the first Macclesfield born man to represent England at cricket when he was picked to play against the formidable West Indies at The Oval. Sadly his Test match career was short lived and finished with an appearance against Australia in Manchester in 1985. In all he represented England in three test matches against Australia and the West Indies and three one day internationals against India and Australia, taking 7 wickets in total; a disappointing return from a promising fast bowler.

Strangely, although his international career appeared to end in 1985, his best seasons were still to come. In 1987 he took 101 wickets in the season for Leicestershire, an amazing performance for which he was nominated by Wisden as one of their five best cricketers for 1988. It was also in 1988 that his future path was decreed when he wrote a book called *8 Days a Week* that was a warts and all insight into the life of a professional cricketer. It was a stark, honest representation of a life bereft of glamour. Continually on the road, dingy bed and breakfast places, no time to spare and boredom with some day's play washed out and, of course, very little money. Trying to find jobs when the season ended was a continual nightmare. He did a whole variety of jobs including lorry driving before, in 1987, shrewdly gaining some media experience working off-season with BBC Radio Leicester as a sports producer. In 1990 he was offered a role at *Today* as a cricket correspondent and decided finally to retire from first-class cricket at the relatively early age of 30. Sadly the new job didn't last when the paper became defunct. However, in 1991 the BBC offered him a job as a cricket correspondent and very soon he found himself working alongside broadcasting legends such as Henry Blofeld, Bill Frindall and of course Brian Johnston on *Test Match Special* a long established favourite programme of cricket lovers. Although very much a junior figure 'Aggers' was well accepted and quickly started to learn from the experienced team.

He was party to one of the most pleasurable broadcasting moments in August 1991, when commentating with Brian Johnston during the England v West Indies Test Match. They became helpless and reduced to fits of giggles and tears following a chance remark by 'Aggers'. Ian Botham was batting and in trying to avoid a fast ball he knocked down his wickets and was given out. Agnew made the now historic comment "He just couldn't quite get his leg over", a statement known to most as a sexual euphemism. Johnston started to giggle while Agnew manfully tried to carry on with the commentary with his voice breaking up then going higher and higher as he struggled to talk without giggling. Johnston tried to take over while Agnew collapsed in the box into a fit of giggles. Eventually Johnston implored "Aggers, for goodness sake do stop it", before dissolving into more giggles. They were like two naughty schoolboys giggling at a piece of smut. It was a delicious moment of human frailty and was voted the greatest piece of sporting commentary by BBC Radio 5 Live. 'Aggers' had arrived.

Although he was very happy learning his craft in the media, he was asked in 1992 to play for Leicestershire during an emergency when they were having difficulty in fielding a team for the Natwest Trophy semi-final. He performed very well bowling 12 overs and taking 1-31, the onus very much on keeping the runs down. However this small successful taste did not tempt him into returning to the playing field; he was more than happy with his new role.

In 1993 he was voted Sony Sports Reporter of The Year. It was however the death of his great friend and mentor Brian Johnston in 1994 that led to him being offered the job as the BBC's Cricket Correspondent. The rookie had now reached the top of the tree. Jonathan Agnew has been able to maintain this highly popular programme's reputation for relaxed, warm, almost off the cuff informality, so beloved of cricket's listeners and is a very worthy successor to the much beloved and missed Brian Johnston.

He published his second book *Over to You Aggers* in 1997 and writes for newspaper columns and the *Radio Times.* Although he loves his job, he admitted that travelling meant much time spent away from his family was the downside. When asked in the early summer of 2005 what his greatest ambition was, he replied it would be commentating when England managed to beat Australia and regain the Ashes. His prayers were answered just a few weeks later when England regained the Ashes from the touring Australians and he was broadcasting with *Test Match Special.*

Jonathan Agnew is much respected in the world of broadcasting and although he is intrinsically linked with *Test Match Special* he is an ambassador on call to promote the game he loves.

Today he lives in Leicestershire with wife Margaret and their two daughters.

A son of Macclesfield who not only played for his country but also made a success of his media career.

Peter Moores – England Cricket Coach, 2007

Yet another Maxonian underlining our cricketing heritage is Peter Moores, born in the town on 18th December, 1962. His parents Bernard and Winifred had a large Catholic family that included five boys and three girls! It was rather crowded but it was a happy family household in the small cottage on Chester Road. Peter recalled playing cricket with a tennis ball with his brothers in the small back yard and further down the road at Christ Church School playground up against the concrete wall. It is an area that was familiar to me, as part of my upbringing was in Chester Road and I went to Christ Church School and played in that yard many times! The boys were competitive and there was always somebody to play with. However it was at King's School in 1974 when Peter really started to develop as a cricketer after receiving a book by England's wicketkeeper Alan Knott on the art of wicket keeping for his 12th birthday. Peter confessed many years later that it was this book that really focussed his mind on cricket. He was in the school first team at the age of 14 as a wicket-keeper batsman. In 1981 he captained the school team and amassed 980 runs for the season – a phenomenal achievement. After term time Peter played at Macclesfield Cricket Club learning from the more experienced members and always, it seemed, encouraged by his father Bernard. When the time came to leave King's School Peter had the choice to either go to Durham University or to accept a place on the MCC's groundstaff and elected to pursue his heart and seek out a career in the cricket world.

It was as a 21 year old that he made his professional county cricket debut playing and keeping wicket for Worcestershire in 1983. Two years later he made the move which would define his career progression and moved to Sussex. He was awarded his county cap in 1989 and made captain in 1997. However, in 1998, he took the decision to retire from playing county cricket after a career embracing fifteen years with 7000 runs scored and over 500 wicketkeeper victims to take up the role as Chief Coach at Sussex. Success was almost immediate when the following season Sussex won the Second Division National Cricket League title under his influence.

In 2000-01 he was appointed coach to the England A team on its tour of the West Indies, his first taste on the international stage. In the summer Sussex won promotion from the Second Division of the County Championship to the First Division. Two years later Sussex were County Champions for the first time in their history. Quite clearly Peter Moores had a penchant for coaching and influencing players, perhaps beyond his own ability.

Further honours came his way and, in 2005, just after he had made the shortlist as coach of the West Indies he was appointed director to the National Cricket Centre, a most coveted role that clearly identified him with the ability and potential for greater roles.

In 2007, following a series of disappointing results, England parted company with their Zimbabwean cricket coach, Duncan Fletcher. Peter Moores finally reached the pinnacle and was appointed coach to the England Cricket Team. When the news reached the Macclesfield streets it was said that his brothers congregated at their local, the Chester Road Tavern, and raised their glasses to him.

Peter's first 18 months in charge had been unpredictable – some good performances, some poor, with the drama of Michael Vaughan resigning in tears during a media interview and the coming of new skipper Kevin Pieterson with five successive victories. Good judges believed that Peter Moores was a good motivator, strong on self-discipline, insistent on a keen work ethic and tough as required; the right qualities for the demanding role. His elevation to high celebrity status had no effect on his demeanour. Although he lives with wife Karen and their two children in a little village just outside Loughborough, he has great affection for Macclesfield. Oldest brother Tony, Peter's first coach, is still a member of Macclesfield Cricket Club, while elder brother Steve is first team cricket coach at King's School.

Following his appointment as England Cricket Coach, Peter told the Macclesfield Express "What's great for me is that when I come back to Macclesfield, loads of my friends and family are there. I see people I grew up with and go down to the club. My time at King's and growing up in Macclesfield was just fantastic". You can take the boy out of Macclesfield but you can't take Macclesfield out of the boy. Peter Moores appears to be a well-grounded person whose values are clear, with an appreciation of where he comes from.

Real success in his new role very much depended on forging a strong bond with captain Kevin Pieterson. Sadly, in January 2009, Peter Moores was sacked from his England post following a series of disappointing results and lurid headlines suggesting that all was not well in the England camp. It was later confirmed that behind the scenes the captain Kevin Pieterson and coach Peter Moores had for some time endured an uneasy relationship, with Pieterson having little faith in Moores experience and ability as an international coach. The English Cricket Board investigated the various issues and indeed interviewed several of the England squad in an effort to resolve the issue. Plainly most pundits were of the opinion that you cannot have the England captain dictating to the cricket board and selecting the coach himself. Following their investigation the English Cricket Board controversially sacked Peter Moores and Pieterson was virtually forced to resign.

In February 2009 Peter Moores regained his self-esteem when accepting the appointment as Head Coach of Lancashire County Cricket Club.

Soccer

Chris Nicholl – Northern Ireland International

Chris Nicholl has the distinction of being the first Macclesfield born footballer to play international soccer. In a long and distinguished professional playing career from, 1965 to 1984, he played 51 times for Northern Ireland, 1975-84 as a defender, and managed to score three international goals.

Christopher John Nicholl was born by chance in Macclesfield on 12th October, 1946 while his parents were visiting relatives in Wilmslow.

His parents, journey man joiner, John and Merle were living in the Crumlin Road, Belfast at the time and were on a visit to John's parents who lived in Cheshire. The birth was imminent and that's how Macclesfield came to be blessed with its first international footballer.

After the birth the family went back to Belfast, but three years later returned to England and made their home in Wilmslow near to John's grandparents. After attending primary school he went to Wilmslow Grammar School, who did not take kindly to his by then burgeoning soccer talent. At the age of 16 he signed for Burnley and travelled from Wilmslow into Manchester and from Manchester by train to Burnley for training sessions.

He played for two seasons (1963-65) in the youth team but sadly only made one first team appearance in a testimonial match before moving to play for Witton Albion in the Cheshire League in 1966. He made little impact at Witton and in 1968 transferred to Halifax Town where at last he was given an opportunity to establish himself. After an excellent season in which he made more than 40 appearances and in which Halifax finished runners up in the Fourth Division to achieve promotion, he was spotted and signed by Luton Town. He spent three seasons at Luton, managing to score three goals in 97 games for the 'Hatters', before once again moving on. However his next move to Aston Villa would define his career. He signed for the Villa in 1972 and, in his first season, the club won the Third Division Championship and started their ascendancy into the top flight of English league soccer. 1975 was a particularly eventful year in his career; Villa won the Football League Cup (and did so again in 1977 with Chris as captain) and Chris achieved the distinction of winning his first international cap against Sweden, and on his debut, he scored a goal! Chris could have played for England, by nature of his birth, but chose to play for Northern Ireland, the birthplace and home of his parents.

In 1976 he achieved an extremely rare feat and one which has become, over the years, 'a must' in any sports quiz. 'Who scored all four goals in March 1976 in the Aston Villa v Leicester City, 2-2 draw?' Answer: Chris Nicholl, of course, two own goals and two against the opposition quite a day – quite a feat!

His international career was thriving when, after more than 200 games for Aston Villa, he signed in 1977 for Southampton and once again enjoyed a modicum of success when in 1979 the team finished runners up in the Football League Cup Final. He left Southampton after 228 matches for the club and joined Grimsby Town in 1983, where he made 70 appearances in three seasons. His international career also came to an end in 1983 with a match against Turkey; he was later acclaimed as one of Northern Ireland's most popular and respected players. During his international career Chris appeared seven times against England.

In 1985, he retired from playing and returned to First Division Southampton as manager following Lawrie McMenemy's resignation. The team had Danny Wallace, Mathew Le Tissier and Alan Shearer in the squad but after six seasons success was sporadic – just two semi-final losses in the FA Cup and League Cup, both to Liverpool in 1986 and 1987. After a poor season in 1991 Nicholl was sacked and it was three seasons later that he came back into the game as manager of Walsall in 1994. His first season in charge was successful and the club were promoted from Division Three as runners-up. However, despite having two more relatively successful seasons, Nicholl resigned as manager in 1997 believed to have been prompted by family troubles. He was tempted back to the club by Ray Graydon in November 2001 as his assistant but resigned again when, only three months later, Graydon was sacked.

Despite this seesaw relationship, when the club was in trouble in February 2006 following the sacking of manager Paul Merson, Nicholl offered to step into the breech but was not given the opportunity to take over as full time manager.

Chris Nicholl still lives in the Walsall area and still attends home matches and enjoys his role as sports correspondent for PA Sport.

Chris Nicholl, Macclesfield's first ever international footballer, played at the highest professional level winning several coveted trophies and also enjoyed respect as a soccer club manager. It is a testimony to his professionalism that several of the clubs that he was connected to during his time were happy to welcome him back into their ranks at various levels.

Lee Dixon – England International

Lee Dixon was born in Manchester on 17th March, 1964 and the family moved to Styal when he was eight years old. He was educated at Wilmslow Grammar School and when he left at the age of 16 he enrolled at Macclesfield College of Further Education, where he studied economics. In the meantime he worked at his father's meat factory where part of his job was cleaning the cellars, for which he earned the princely sum of £25 per week.

He had a talent for soccer and started playing in the local Macclesfield leagues. It was during his sixth season playing for Priory County FC that his ability was recognised and he was signed to play for Burnley youths in 1983. He alternated his time between Burnley and the local leagues and then he had spells with Chester City, Bury and finally Stoke. It was during his time with Stoke that Arsenal recognised something that the others had missed and paid £350,000 for him in January 1988. Just a few weeks later in February he made the first appearance of what would be very many over a highly successful career embracing almost twenty years. When Arsenal signed him he admitted that he couldn't believe his luck and thought to himself "How did that happen?"

During Arsenal's highly successful period from the late 1980s and all through the 1990s, Lee played in more than 600 matches as a fast, hard attacking right full back. His honours came thick and fast; League titles in 1988/9, 1990/91, 1997/98, 2001/2, FA Cup winner 1993, 1998 and 2002, League Cup 1993, Charity Shield in 1998, European Cup Winners 1994 and runners up in 1995. It will be seen from the record that uniquely Lee Dixon was part of an Arsenal team that on two occasions achieved the very rare distinction of performing the football double, i.e. winning the Football League title as well as the FA Cup in the same seasons. He was an integral part of an Arsenal defence, rated one of the best in Football League history.

He received his first cap for England against Czechoslovakia in 1990 and went on to represent his country 22 times. His long, successful soccer career came to an end when after Arsenal again won the double in 2001/2 he decided to retire. He was 38, old for a top soccer player but an indication of how fit and astute Dixon had been throughout his career ensuring that he was able to continue and to earn the large wages available long beyond the span of the average league player.

Although he was living and, of course, playing for most of his career in the south he did make frequent visits to the Cheshire area to old friends in Macclesfield and to his wife's family, who lived in Knutsford and Congleton.

After retirement at such a young age and with no desire to continue in the soccer industry, he pursued his interest in food by investing in a friend's chain of restaurants.

Classically they expanded too quickly without the requisite control and went bust causing Dixon to lose his investment. However, following a visit to Bray, Berkshire and lunch at the Riverside Brasserie he was persuaded by a friend to invest in the business along with celebrity chef, Heston Blumenthal. Today it is still a going concern and helps keep Lee involved. He is also involved in a property venture helping relocate footballers following transfers to new clubs and owns property in Penzance and Santa Monica, California.

However he achieved a real breakthrough for an alternative career when he appeared as a pundit on the BBC's *Match of The Day* along with Alan Hansen, Gary Linekar and Mark Lawrenson in 2004 and today is still a regular on the team.

He is an avid golf fanatic and plays off a handicap of five and is considering starting a golf-oriented business where businessmen would play golf with prominent sportsmen. He told an interviewer that his ambition is to play golf at the highest level as he enjoys the one on one feeling of intense competition. Sadly no longer married his varied interests keep him busy.

Lee Dixon certainly seems to have made the most of his opportunities and it is enlightening to know that the foundations of his career were laid in Macclesfield. Perhaps the astute way in which he has managed his interests can in some way be attributed to the training he received at the Macclesfield College of Further Education.

Peter Crouch – England International
Born on 30th January, 1981, Peter James Crouch, to parents James Bruce Crouch, an advertising writer and Jayne Elizabeth Crouch of Holly Cottage, 199 London Road, Poynton became the first Macclesfield born footballer ever to play for England. His other distinction is that he is the tallest player, at 6 feet 7inches, ever to be capped by England.

However, when he was a toddler the family moved to London and then, at the age of four, the family moved to Singapore before returning to England and Ealing, London just eighteen months later.

Peter Crouch

As a schoolboy he was tall and skinny yet displayed an outstanding aptitude for soccer. As a youngster he was a ballboy at Chelsea, his father's favourite club, and they tried to sign him when he was twelve years old. However, he ended up at Tottenham Hotspur as a trainee but never actually played for the first team. It was Queens Park Rangers who eventually signed him and in his first and only season with QPR he scored ten goals in 38 matches and was capped by the England Under-21 team. His success attracted the attention of Harry Redknapp, the manager of Portsmouth, who signed the 20-year-old centre forward for £1.25 million. In a brilliant first season he scored 18 goals in only 37 games and Graham Taylor, the former England manager and then manager of Aston Villa, paid Portsmouth £5 million for Crouch in 2002. It was good business for Portsmouth, making a huge profit, and it increased Crouch's profile amongst the soccer elite. However his three season spell at Aston Villa was disappointing and he even spent a spell at Norwich on loan.

His world turned upside down when, in July 2004, Southampton signed the twenty three year old and again he returned to the south coast. There were many who thought that his career had peaked and that his early promise would not be fulfilled.

Peter disproved the doubters with an excellent spell at Southampton scoring 17 goals in one season and attracting the attention of England. He was selected for the England USA tour and on 31st May, 2005 received his first England cap against Columbia in New Jersey. He played target man to the diminutive Michael Owen who scored a hat-trick.

Liverpool were alerted to his talents – obviously his height gives him a distinct advantage – as a tall target man being able to knock balls down from the air to let in fellow strikers or, of course, attacking balls sent in from the wings or from dead kick situations. However, Crouch for a big man, is surprisingly skilful with the ball at his feet. These attributes led Liverpool, in July 2005, to pay £7 million pounds for the former 'Macc' lad! 2005 was a memorable year for him and three more England caps came his way against Austria, Poland and Argentina.

Peter Crouch quickly became a highly popular figure at Anfield – the fans recognised that here was a totally committed player and, despite constant criticism from some quarters, he always gave of his best. After a slow start, he started to make goals and scored 6 himself, winning over the fans. In 2006, he played in the European Champions League and was selected for the England World Cup squad. He scored his first England goal against Uruguay, fittingly at Anfield, and scored a hat-trick against Jamaica and scored again in the World Cup against Paraguay. However, despite his success, Benitez the Liverpool manager signed Fernando Torres the excellent Spanish international centre forward for more than £20 million. Although many thought that they might make an excellent partnership, with the tall ball-playing Crouch laying off balls for the very swift Spanish forward, Benitez preferred to play Torres up front on his own. Sadly Peter Crouch began to find himself more and more on the bench and playing in the less important matches or coming on for twenty minutes or so. His chances became few and far between, his form suffered and he lost his place in the England team.

In 2008 came the opportunity to resurrect his career, when former boss Harry Redknapp paid Liverpool £11 million for the services of his former player.

Liverpool actually offered Crouch a contract for the 2008 season and did not want to let him go. However, although Crouch did not want to leave Liverpool, did not want to accept a large salary and faint praise for winning trophies that he actually hadn't earned or languish on the bench. He wanted to play to regain his England place.

In his time at Liverpool he scored 40 goals in 135 games and won a FA Cup winners medal and, in 2007, a European Champions League runners up medal.

Many Liverpool fans were sorry to see him leave Anfield and the *Liverpool Echo* newspaper was very complimentary and reflected the views of many of the fans when they said how impressed they had been with his loyalty, stating that he had made "the most dignified of goodbyes". Crouch told the newspapers "What a great club to have played for. I have only got fond memories of my time there". He recalled some great moments, winning the FA Cup, scoring a hat-trick against Arsenal, a brilliant scissor kick goal in the European Champions League match against Galatasaray in 2006, knocking Manchester United out of the FA Cup and getting to the European Champions League Final by beating Chelsea in the semi-finals.

Nevertheless, despite great memories, he returned to Portsmouth for the second time in his career and formed a very potent strike force with another England striker Jermain Defoe who had also transferred to Portsmouth from Tottenham.

Crouch's scoring record for England is a highly respectable 14 goals in 28 matches; only 14 of which he played in for the full period. In 2010 his England career continued to flourish.

He is now living on the south coast and has a regular girlfriend, Liverpool model Abbey Clancy, who in September 2008 appeared on the Jonathan Ross show praising her boyfriend and commented that whenever they are out together men always want to talk to Peter rather than chat her up, but she understood as he was so popular.

In the 2009 season his career turned full circle when former Portsmouth manager Harry Redknapp, after moving to take over as manager of Tottenham Hotspur, signed Crouch for the Spurs in yet another multi-million pound transfer. Crouch returned to the club who had signed him as a junior but never played him.

Peter remembers his roots and when he returns to Macclesfield on occasions he calls in at the Prince of Wales pub, Porters in Roe Street and when Macclesfield Town FC were threatened with bankruptcy he obtained a signed Liverpool shirt to be raffled for the fighting fund to meet the £300,000 fine imposed on the club by the FA.

I think that Peter Crouch will continue to be successful and will continue to add to his England honours for some time to come.

Rugby Union

Steve Smith – Captain of England

Prestbury born FG Handforth was the first local person to play for England at rugby (as detailed in the chapter on King's School) and, although several players have played for Cheshire without question Steve Smith, in modern times, is the greatest rugby player to have been produced by this town.

Although not Macclesfield born – he was born in Stockport in 1951 – Steve was educated at King's School and spent six years from 1962-68 travelling every day to Macclesfield.

He started to show great promise as a rugby player at King's and was soon earning several honours at junior level.

After leaving King's he went to Loughborough University where he met a young man called Fran Cotton and they both played rugby for Loughborough University.

Steve returned to Cheshire and played for Wilmslow and Sale but very soon more senior honours came his way. He was selected for Lancashire and the North of England before gaining his first England cap at scrum half. He started to tour the world with the 1970s England team that also featured Fran Cotton. For the next ten years his career blossomed. However, it was during the era when rugby was amateur and a living had to be made outside the game.

He had a most successful England career earning 28 caps and becoming England's most capped scrum half. He had the distinction of captaining his country and was a member of the all-conquering 1980 England team that won the Grand Slam, i.e. beating all four nations, France, Scotland, Ireland and Wales in the annual championship. He was also a member of the England seven that won the centenary international sevens at Murrayfield.

However, perhaps his greatest accolade was to be selected for the British Lions Tour of New Zealand in 1983 and captaining the team against Hawkes Bay.

During his England career Steve also trained as a teacher of physical education and he taught for a time at West Cheshire College. In 1981 he joined, along with Fran Cotton, Bukta Sportswear and very quickly the pair became joint Managing Directors and in 1983 sold the company to French Connection.

In 1987, Steve and Fran started a company called Cotton Traders Ltd producing sports wear, stylish and hard-wearing rugby shirts and

Leading England out at Twickenham

general sports attire sold by mail order. Steve was Wholesale Director and Fran was Managing Director, responsible for marketing.

In addition to this business, which is still running today, Steve has maintained his interest in rugby as a commentator and presenter for ITV covering internationals and World Cups and was a proud member of the commentary team covering England winning the World Cup in 2003.

Steve and his family live in Altrincham and he has been an integral part of rugby in this area all his life. Interestingly his business partner, England legend Fran Cotton who lives in Macclesfield with his family, is also still very active in rugby circles. Indeed, in 1997, he

Steve Smith, businessman

managed the British Lions Touring Team that won in South Africa and is a member of the Rugby Union Management Board and was chairman of the Club England Committee responsible for the England World Cup winning side of 2003.

Golf

Jamie Donaldson

Macclesfield can lay claim to one of the country's top professional golfers. Although Jamie Donaldson was born in Pontypridd, Wales he has spent most of his life in Macclesfield and indeed nurtured his golf career whilst living in the town.

Jamie came to Macclesfield with his family in 1984 when he was aged 9. He grew up in Ryles Park Road, where his parents still live and went to school firstly at Ashgrove Primary School and then Henbury High. He started to play golf around the age of 11 at Macclesfield Golf

Club and his burgeoning talent started to win him a number of amateur trophies. After leaving Henbury High at the age of 16 his first job was working as an assistant at a golf shop in the Marlborough Court precinct off Pickford Street. However this job was the first step in his ambition to become a golf professional and he continued to impress in amateur tournaments, picking up several titles.

In 1997 he was extremely proud to win the Welsh Amateur Championship but the pivotal year in his career came in 2000. He won the Welsh Amateur Open Stroke Play Championship, represented Wales in the Eisenhower Trophy and after representing Great Britain and Ireland in the St Andrews Trophy decided to turn professional and joined the Challenge Tour. In 2001 he was also appointed Academy Director and Head Professional at the PGA Professional Golfers Association, whom he has represented at the British Open and Ryder Cup since 2001. His first year as a touring professional in 2001 was successful. He won the Russian Open and the Telia Grand Prix in Sweden and ended the year in second place in the Challenge Tour Rankings list – a highly satisfying first season. His performances propelled him into the main European Tour where he tried to become established. Sadly a spinal condition plagued him for some time and he was unable to compete and give of his best. In 2005 he was able to attain two top ten finishes in tournaments. His form suffered but an example of Jamie's potential was demonstrated in the Dubai Desert Classic in 2006 at the sumptuous Emirates Golf Club. At the end of the first day he shared the lead with Retief Goosen, one of the world's leading players, on 64 with a certain gentleman called Tiger Woods three strokes behind on 67. The extremely warm desert conditions were beneficial for Jamie's back condition where the often chilly, damp conditions on Britain's golf courses don't. He also achieved a considerable milestone in 2006 by qualifying for the British Open at Royal Liverpool and Arighi Bianchi sponsored a shirt deal for him.

Despite this glimpse of what could be, Jamie's performances dipped below his expectations and saw him relegated to the Challenge Tour in 2007. However, once again he acquitted himself well on the tour with six top four finishes and ended the season in 4th place; the highlight being his third major championship victory, winning the Abierto Telefonica de Guatemala. His excellent performances once again earned him the much-coveted right to play on the European Tour in 2008.

Despite the handicap caused by his back condition, Jamie completed more than 15 tournaments in 2008 and at the year -end had achieved three top ten finishes; a highly credible 10th place in July in the European Open and in August an 8th place in the SAS Scandinavian Open. He finished the year in style when winning, in December, the Mauritius Golf Open Championship defeating the French favourite Gregory Havret.

Jamie Donaldson in full swing

He is currently ranked in the top 100 players in Europe and one feels that if only he could get a period free from the back problem that plagues him he could become an even more high profile player on the world circuit.

In April 2009 he led going into the last round of the Estoril Open de Portugal but finished two shots behind the eventual winner. It was the sixth time in eight tournaments that Jamie had made the 'cut' in the season, a testament to his increasing consistency. As 2009 continued and Jamie was having fewer problems with his back, his results continued to be impressive. Runner up in the Swedish SAS Masters, 5th in the KLM Dutch Open, just two shots off the winner and 6th in the Johnnie Walker Championship at Gleneagles gave him impressive earnings for the season.

In 2010 a regime of twice daily back massages helped him to his best ever season. In April he won £67,000 when finishing 4th in the China Open and followed that in June with a joint 6th place in the Madrid Masters and a cheque for £38,000. During this period he enjoyed five top ten finishes in six tournaments but excelled himself when finishing joint 3rd at the Johnny Walker Championships at Gleneagles on 29th August. In august company he revealed his true potential when finishing equal third with Ryder Cup 2010 selections Italian Francesco Molinari and Spaniard Miguel Jimenex and beating two other members of the European Ryder Cup team Peter Hanson of Sweden and England's Ross Fisher.

Jamie Donaldson has proved himself amongst the best golfers in the world and Macclesfield and Wales can be extremely proud of him.

Scientists, Soldiers and Explorers

Scientists

Professor Sir James Chadwick, MSc, PhD, FRS – Physicist
Clarke Lane, Bollington is the birthplace of one of this country's greatest scientists. James Chadwick was born there on 20th October, 1891 to John Joseph Chadwick and Anne Mary Chadwick. Born into poor circumstances, his father was a cotton spinner, James was a bright, shy lad but he was quick to learn. While still very young his father and mother left the family home to run a laundry business in Manchester, leaving young James to be supervised by his grandmother. He attended local schools before eventually moving to be nearer his parents and entering the Manchester Municipal Secondary School. In 1908 his promise was evident when he gained two scholarships in applied mathematics and entered Owens College, later expanded to become Manchester University. Although his forte was mathematics it is said that he was so shy that he did not correct a mistaken interviewer who believed that he was applying for a physics placement. Chadwick however allowed the error to stand and started to study physics. It would be mankind who would benefit enormously from this so basic of errors, this twist of fate.

In Manchester he worked with the legendary Professor Ernest Rutherford, the discoverer of the nucleus, and soon received his First Class Honours and in 1913 received his Masters Degree. Rutherford recommended him for a scholarship specialising in radioactivity, but he decided to leave Manchester and go with German scientist Geiger to study at the Technische Hochschule, Reichsanstalt in Berlin. During this eventful time Geiger introduced the young Chadwick to Albert Einstein. Sadly this highly interesting period in his life was interrupted by the outbreak of the First World War. Geiger was called away to serve in the German army and Chadwick was interned and imprisoned in an old stable with five others in very trying conditions. It was very cold and the supply of food was both sparse and inadequate.

After four years of imprisonment and poor health, mercifully the war was ended and he was released and on his return to England was offered a job by Rutherford. Later Rutherford accepted the post of Cavendish professor at Cambridge and invited Chadwick to join him

Professor Sir James Chadwick (courtesy of University of Liverpool)

and help run the Cavendish Laboratory. In 1921 he obtained his PhD and in 1922 was appointed Assistant Director of Research in the Cavendish. His role was purely research reporting to Professor Rutherford with whom he worked very closely.

In 1925 James Chadwick married Aileen Stewart-Brown, a Liverpool girl. Their first house together was still being refurbished when they moved in and Chadwick, who was studying and revising Rutherford's book on radioactivity, had to study wearing an overcoat and gloves: it was déjà vu back to his Berlin incarceration!

In 1927 he became a Fellow of the Royal Society and in 1928 was awarded the Royal Medal of the Royal Society. His work and talent was being recognised on a wider scale.

However his major discovery occurred in 1930. Rutherford and Chadwick had believed that there was a type of neutral particle still to be discovered and had for the past ten years experimented in an effort to isolate it without success. It was Chadwick, with his painstaking research, who discovered the particle, 'neutron', opening the doors to the development of nuclear fission: it was a discovery that would change the world. During this time Chadwick had along with Geiger and Ellis published a book, *Radiation from Radioactive Substances*, that would prove invaluable in what was to come. He had a keen interest in radio-activity and became one of the world's leading experts.

In 1935 Professor James Chadwick received the ultimate accolade awarded in his field when he received the Nobel Laureate Prize in Physics.

Chadwick was anxious to further his research and wanted to build a more powerful accelerator at Cambridge. After Rutherford refused his request, saying it was too expensive, Chadwick moved to accept the Lyon Jones Chair of Physics at Liverpool University. He also moved house to Denbigh, North Wales with his wife and twin daughters.

He quickly built up the run down physics department at Liverpool and started to build a cyclotron but sadly had a falling out with Rutherford over who was to design it, which dampened their friendship for a time. Sadly they had just returned to a friendly basis when, in 1937, Rutherford, one of the great scientists of his day died.

The Liverpool cyclotron was operational just as the Second World War broke out. Uranium fission had been discovered, revealing that there was a possibility of a nuclear chain reaction. The British

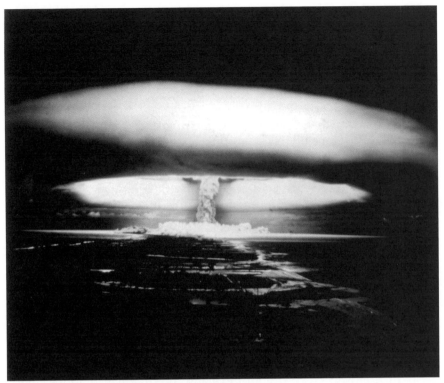

Atom bomb (courtesy of Imperial War Museum)

government asked Chadwick if it were possible to build a nuclear bomb but Chadwick was uncertain, as more than a ton of uranium would be required to detonate a device: he agreed to use the Liverpool cyclotron for a feasibility study. His work revealed that the American researchers had overestimated the amount of uranium needed to set off a chain reaction and along with others reported that a nuclear bomb could be developed by 1943.

It was agreed that American and British scientists would work together and from 1943-46 James Chadwick headed the British Mission working in Los Alamos on atomic weapons, the Manhattan Project. They were successful – extremely so – and were responsible for ending the Second World War. He ensured total cooperation between the British and American scientists to achieve the finalisation of the project. On 6th August, 1945, America dropped an atom bomb on Hiroshima that would eventually kill more than 200,000 people and then on 9th August after Chadwick selected British observers to witness the event, they dropped another bomb on Nagasaki killing more than 75,000 people. Although this cost of human life was barbaric, Japan sued for peace four days later and by shortening the war it perhaps saved many more lives, as Japan had shown no intention of surrendering.

The war over, he returned mentally shattered and was knighted in 1945 for his service to the country. America awarded him the US Medal of Merit in 1946 and he received a whole string of international honours. For a time he worked on the British nuclear energy programme, advised the British delegation to the United Nations in 1947 and set about making a new synchrocyclotron at Liverpool so that when he left in 1948 it was the biggest outside the United States.

For a time he was at the centre of European scientific issues before, in 1948, surprisingly moving to Cambridge to become Master of Gonville and Caius College. Although he missed actively working on research in the laboratory, he enjoyed the interface with students. In 1950 he was awarded the prestigious Faraday Medal for his services to science.

After ten years, in 1958, he had had enough of university politics and retired to a cottage in North Wales. He continued to work on and off in his beloved Liverpool and in 1969 the Chadwick's moved back to Cambridge to be closer to their two daughters.

Professor Sir James Chadwick, Nobel Prize winner and Bollington lad, died in Cambridge in July 1974.

Dr Alexander Rawson Stokes

A Macclesfield born scientist, Alexander Stokes was, most scientists believe, very unlucky not to receive a Nobel Laureate prize and many believe strongly that he should have been awarded the ultimate accolade.

He was born in Macclesfield at Glen View, Hurdsfield Road on 27th June, 1919. His father George William Stokes was an architect and his mother was Amelia Farmer.

Stokes attended local schools before moving on to Cheadle Hulme school near Manchester and from there he went to Trinity College, Cambridge and started work in the Cavendish Laboratories where Chadwick and Rutherford had gone before. He was a gifted student and very soon he completed his PhD in x-ray crystallography.

However, his real expertise was in mathematics and he applied his techniques to crystallographic analysis.

At the end of the war in 1945 he was a lecturer in physics at the Royal Holloway College in Surrey. His unique skills were evident when he published a paper in 1946 on the construction and use of a 'fly's eye' for assisting X-ray structure analysis. In this case the 'fly's eye' is a multiple, using lenses embossed on Perspex that would give two-dimensional diffraction gratings of repeated patterns representing projections of crystal structures. The effect was that a beam of light was forced to spread when meeting a narrow opening caused by parallel bars (gratings). It was also during this time, 1946, that Stokes married his wife Margaret and together they would raise a family of two sons and a daughter.

His reputation as a mathematician was such that he was asked to join John Randall's team at King's College, London. The team comprised biologists and biochemists whose brief was to work with physicists in order to understand more fully the structure of complex biological molecules like DNA by using diffraction photographs, a field that Stokes was very adept in.

DNA pioneers (1953), left to right: *Raymond Gosling, Herbert Wilson, Maurice Wilkins, Dr ALex Stokes (courtesy of King's College, London)*

But Stokes particular expertise was in mathematics and it was this skill that was so vital in being able to translate the patterns created on X-ray diffraction film into a description of the atoms that must have produced them.

By this time several scientists were engaged in the hunt, the search for the construction of DNA. Francis Crick and James Watson were working at Cambridge University but Stokes joined the team of Maurice Wilkins and Rosalind Franklin who had been researching well before Crick and Watson.

In 1950 the first major breakthrough occurred when, in an experiment, Wilkins obtained a long thread of DNA from a solution and then subjected it to X-ray which revealed a clear pattern of spots indicating a shape. However, excited as he was, he still did not know what he was looking for and so he turned to Stokes and his mathematical expertise. Stokes was able to reveal that what they were looking at was the diffraction pattern of a helix, in the shape of a ladder. The story goes that Alexander Stokes produced the diagram with the all-important shape overnight! In the meantime Watson was on the trail but was discouraged by several false indications.

What was eventually undisputed was Stokes mathematical genius that helped the other scientists to recognise the shape they were looking for, which helped Crick and Watson to build a three-dimensional model showing that DNA was shaped like a spiral ladder. They acknowledged that the work of Stokes, Wilkins and Franklin describing the evidence provided by X-ray diffraction photographs of DNA fibres had been crucial in their discovery of the structure of DNA, the biological molecule that carries our genetic identity.

In 1962, Francis Crick and James Watson of Cambridge University and Maurice Wilkins of King's College, London received the Nobel Prize for physiology and medicine. Alexander Stokes, whom they all acknowledged had set them on the final path to success, went unrecognised, apart from the praise of his colleagues.

Identifying the biological molecule that carries our genetic identity was a massive discovery, unquestionably the most important discovery in biological research of the century. It will come in time to be regarded as the most vital discovery in the history of genetic research and in the future of mans existence.

The modest Stokes continued his work into research on light, prisms, and X-ray scattering of chain molecules throughout the 1950s and 1960s. He was also senior lecturer at King's College, London and eventually retired in 1982.

During his career he wrote many papers and several books including *The Principles of Atomic and Nuclear Physics* and, the wonderfully titled, *The Theory of the Optical Properties of Inhomogeneous Materials.*

In 1993, a plaque was installed at King's College, London listing the names of those, including Stokes, who had been involved in the 1953 project of the X- ray study that led to the discovery of the structure of DNA; Stokes was there to enjoy the moment but he should have had so much more.

He had a long and happy retirement indulging his hobbies of playing the piano and singing in the choir at his local Free Church in Welwyn Garden City.

Dr Alexander Rawson Stokes, a Macclesfield man, who should have received the Nobel Prize, died in February 2003 aged 83, survived by his wife, two sons and daughter.

Dr Michael Dexter FRS

Dr Mike Dexter was born in Manchester on 15th May, 1945 to Thomas Richard Dexter and Agnes Gertrude Depledge. His education commenced at Ducie Avenue Primary School and then, after he spurned an offer to go to Manchester Grammar School, he elected to go to the Central Grammar School, Manchester. He cheerfully admits that after suffering viral pneumonia for several months he flopped his A levels and decided to drop out. It was the 1960s!

For a time he pursued the 1960s dream, folk singing and undertaking hedonistic studies, the pursuit of pleasure for the uninitiated, before eventually taking a job then leaving it, because it was boring.

The pivotal moment in his life came when he became a laboratory technician in the cancer research laboratories attached to the Christie Hospital, Manchester. Not only was it to become his destiny but also working at the hospital was wife to be, Macclesfield girl, a farmers daughter from Hurdsfield, Frances Ann Sutton. The family farmed at Lower Swanscoe at the bottom of Kerridge Hill.

At this point Mike became inspired and decided to take his A levels and go on to University. This is where the second Macclesfield area connection comes into play; he married Frances in 1966 and moved to Rainow, close by the church. At this time Frances was working at Stockport Hospital as a radiotherapy radiographer and Mike accepted a place at Salford University as a mature student.

Times must have been tough but Mike supported by Frances survived and he fondly recalls many a night trying to supplement his income by playing cards in the Rising Sun pub in Rainow.

At various times over the years he has lived in Disley, Heaton Mersey and Grimshaw Lane, Bollington and recalls, he says with great fondness, playing for the Queens Arms pool team and winter nights with the pub fire roaring up the chimney and free chips.

Sadly his marriage to Frances finished in 1978 but together they had produced a son and a daughter.

Today Mike has a new partner Dr Elaine Spooncer with whom he has another son and another daughter; in 1983 they moved to Adlington, just outside Macclesfield where they still live today.

Within ten years of joining Christies' as a laboratory technician Mike was appointed in 1977 Senior Scientist at the complex which in

Dr Mike Dexter with Chancellor Prince Philip at Cambridge University, 2003

the early 1960s was named after its founder Professor Ralston Paterson. A year later he also joined the Life Fell Cancer Research Campaign, an organisation with which he would be associated with until 1998.

He and his Manchester team were at this time engaged in highly complex research embracing stem cell biology, cell differentiation, gene therapy and intense research into cancer biology.

Dr Dexter was appointed Head of Department into Experimental Haematology at the Paterson Institute for Cancer Research in 1982, a post he held until 1998, and Professor of Haematology at the University of Manchester in 1985. He was fundamentally engaged in the science of blood disorders.

From 1988-89, he was President of the International Society for Experimental Haematology as his reputation gained huge respect in international scientific circles.

Dexter and his team had made a major breakthrough in the treatment of leukaemia by using blood stem cells grown in a test tube and the process had great success in the treatment of children. The technique, 'Dexter Bone Marrow System' involved growing bone marrow stem cells in the laboratory that were then able to destroy leukaemia cells leaving the surviving healthy cells to be restored to the patient. Mike Dexter deservedly was acclaimed for this discovery and became accepted, and still is, as a world-wide authority in experimental haematology stem cell transportation.

In 1997 he became the Director of the Paterson Institute, the organisation he had joined as a laboratory technician, but held the post for a matter of months when he received an offer he could not refuse. It meant moving to London, when in 1998 he was offered and accepted the post of Director of the Wellcome Trust the largest charitable biomedical research organisation in the world. The post came at a time when valuable research into the human genetic code was being pursed with encouraging results in what was first thought to be an impossible task.

On 26th June, 2000, in London, Dr Mike Dexter was part of an internationally coordinated press release with some amazing news. He informed the waiting press, "I can now reveal one of the best kept secrets ever. (He said it tongue in cheek, as speculation had been rife.)

Today could well be regarded as one of the most significant days in human history. The Human Genome Project has the capacity to impact on every human on Earth. It's better than the invention of the wheel because technology could make that obsolete, the genome never will be."

This first draft of the human genetic code, that initially many thought would never happen, revealed that 97% of the human genetic code had been mapped and 85% of the code was written in the DNA sequence. It was a staggering result and testimony to the several teams working around the world, including the UK.

In March 2003, after five years in this most prominent role, Mike Dexter declined the offer to extend his contract by a further two years and left the Wellcome Trust after a rewarding tenure. He more than doubled the budget during his time and was quick to tackle and criticise the government on lukewarm promises or responses on funds, which he knew were critical to the success and the part that Britain needed to play on the international human genetic code project.

He gave little indication to the press as to what he would do in the future but speculation was rife that it would involve a period of rest back home near Macclesfield. It was known that Mike Dexter returned home to Adlington every weekend while working in London.

Within months however, he accepted the post of Chairman of Stem Cell Sciences and held it until 2006, when he became a non-executive director. In 2004 he accepted the Chair at the Cockroft Institute for Accelerator Science near Warrington and in 2006 he was made an honorary member of Lancaster University.

His awards and accolades are almost too numerous to mention but include honorary degrees at UMIST, University of Salford, University of Newcastle, the Imperial College, London and an award from Thailand. He is a Fellow of the Royal Society, Founder Fellow of the Academy of Medical Sciences and an honorary member of the Royal College of Physicians. He has served, and continues to serve, on a number of medically related bodies and has written more than 360 papers for journals and magazines.

If Dr Mike Dexter is indeed now enjoying a well deserved semi retirement then it is certain that he will be pursuing his hobbies of folk singing, poetry and gardening. He may well remember the old days when playing cards for money in the local pubs and hone up his skills. He is a local man who has left a mark on our society that very many families will come to treasure over the coming years.

Soldiers

Major General John Fielden Brocklehurst
CB, CVO, MVO, Lord Ranksborough, 1st Baron

Macclesfield can be justly proud of one of the most highly regarded and honoured soldiers of the late 19th and early 20th century.

John Fielden Brocklehurst was born into the powerful Macclesfield silk family dynasty on 13th May, 1852 at Foden Bank, Byrons Lane, Macclesfield. His father was Henry Brocklehurst and his grandfather was John Brocklehurst, Macclesfield's first ever MP. His mother, Anne Fielden was the daughter of Oldham's MP 'Honest' John Fielden. He was educated firstly at King's School, Macclesfield before moving on to Rugby and then to Trinity College, Cambridge where he graduated in 1873 with a Bachelor of Arts degree.

He was bent on a career in the military from an early age and, indeed, was commissioned into the Royal Horse Guards in 1874. For a time there were few opportunities for combat action and he did not particularly enjoy the dull day-to-day routine. In 1878 he married Louisa Alice Parsons and although they enjoyed a few short years of wedded bliss, action, worldwide action, would soon envelop them.

It was a frustrating era for the cavalry, who had not been called upon in recent times due to the change in modern warfare, and for a time the cavalry believed that their role was more ceremonial than combative. However, the Anglo-Egyptian War that started in 1882 provided the cavalry with the opportunity, literally to earn their spurs. Brocklehurst was eager for action and was a member of the British forces despatched to put down the Egyptian rebellion. In the Battle of Tel el-Kebir the 17,000 strong British army was outnumbered by the rebels and after fierce fighting in which 2,000 of the enemy were killed, in contrast to 58 British dead, the rebels retreated and surrendered Cairo to the British. The turning point in the battle was due undoubtedly to the advantage gained by the British under Lieutenant General Sir Garnet Wolseley when they force-marched through the night desert to surprise the enemy in the early morning. For his part in the fighting Brocklehurst was mentioned in despatches, rewarded with a war medal and clasp and was awarded the Khedive's bronze star. The campaign concluded in 1884 and the cavalry returned to England triumphant in the role they had played.

When, in 1884, the British organised a force to go to the Sudan and put down the highly dangerous rise of the Mahdi, who had rebelled against the Egyptians and had shocked the Victorian world when his forces massacred an army of 10,000 men led by Colonel William Hicks, Brocklehurst volunteered to fight with the Camel Corps during the Nile Expedition of 1884. He was refused permission but instead was taken on with the Headquarters Staff as Deputy Assistant Adjutant and Quarter Master General and was then promoted as Brevet Major.

The task of the British force was to relieve General Gordon, who was surrounded at Khartoum by the Mahdi's superior forces. Sadly they were too late, after constantly being held up on the journey by fighting with the Mahdi's forces sent deliberately to delay them. When they reached Khartoum, Gordon and his entire garrison had been massacred.

Once again Brocklehurst returned to England but thirsted for adventure; he was appointed Brevet Lieutenant Colonel in 1891.

His marriage to Louisa Alice Parsons was sadly childless but in 1893 they finished the construction of a superb country house, Ranksborough Hall at Langham in County Rutland. It would be the scene of visits by high profile members of the Royal family and politicians, for Brocklehurst was well connected. In 1894 he was made Commander of the Royal Horse Guards, a post that he held until 1899. His integrity and qualities were reflected in other honours, which started to follow: MVO, Member of the Royal Victorian Order and an appointment as equerry to HM Queen Victoria. Despite the pride in recognition, Brocklehurst still thirsted for action and when the Second Boer War broke out in 1899 he once again volunteered for duty. His wish was granted and when he was appointed commander, Major General of the 2nd Cavalry Brigade of the Natal Field Force, he was the youngest to hold such rank.

After heavy fighting, including the battle at Elandslaagte, Brocklehurst commanded his brigade under Lieutenant General French and the British withdrew to the town of Ladysmith which immediately was besieged by the Boers. During the long siege Brocklehurst commanded the Cavalry during several sorties before General Sir Redvers Buller, to the unbridled joy of Victorian England, finally relieved the town. While he was away fighting in South Africa he was invested as a Companion Order of the Bath (CB) in 1900, Commander of the Royal Victorian Order (CVO) in 1901 and was appointed equerry to HM Queen Alexandra, a position he held from 1901-1910.

The war ended in 1902 and on his return to England he was appointed Major General to the 3rd Cavalry Brigade. In 1906 he was made Lord Lieutenant of Rutland, a title he held until his death. In 1908 Major General John Fielden Brocklehurst retired from the army after a very distinguished career having seen action in three historic theatres of war.

However, he was still much in demand and had a whole range of official positions and responsibilities.

In 1914 he was raised to the peerage and became the first Lord Ranksborough, sadly he would also be the last as he had no heir. He took his seat in the House of Lords and, as Baron Ranksborough, he was from 1915-21 the government whip for the Liberal Party serving firstly under HH Asquith and then the legendary David Lloyd George. In 1915 he was appointed Lord in Waiting to his HM King George V.

He died on 28th February, 1921 aged 68, the barony dying with him. Lady Ranksborough died in 1937.

Squadron Leader Dennis Lockhart Armitage DFC

During the many conflicts of the 20th century Maxonians played their part and indeed more than 700 local servicemen gave their lives in battles across the world and many were decorated for their devotion to duty and for their bravery. However I cannot give due recognition to all, but perhaps would single out the men of the Royal Air Force who performed miracles in stopping the invasion of Great Britain during the Battle of Britain in 1940. Flight Sergeant Philip Kirk from Ivy Road, Macclesfield who was reported missing in 1940 but was later found and awarded the Distinguished Flying Medal, Kerridge brothers, Pilot Officers John and Anthony Kershaw both killed and Sergeant Pilot Eric Samuel Bann, a Hurricane fighter pilot killed during the Battle of Britain.

Dennis Armitage was born in Bolton, Lancashire in 1912 but moved to Sutton Hall, Bullocks Lane, Sutton, Macclesfield when he was two or three. The family ran a textile spinning business in Bolton but preferred to live in Cheshire. Dennis was sent away to be educated first at prep school and then at Malvern College and on the completion of his education he worked in the family business. However, he was a young man interested in cars. He had a three-wheeler Morgan, then a 3-litre Bentley and had an early fascination for aeroplanes. He started to learn to fly at local aerodromes and, according to Kevin Whittaker of the Macclesfield Aeronautical Society, Dennis on occasions would return home to Sutton piloting a Tiger Moth and landing in the fields adjacent to Bullocks lane!

In December 1937 he joined the Royal Air Force Voluntary Reserve at Hythe as a pilot airman under training. He eventually completed his training at Brize Norton and commenced full time service on 1st September, 1939. In December 1939 he joined No 266 Squadron and was appointed A Flight Commander on 3rd August, 1940. Later that same month in his Spitfire fighter plane he attacked and destroyed a Junkers JU88 when the Battle of Britain was at its peak. The magnificent 'few' fought off the superior German forces but the loss of life was severe. Dennis or Bill (as he was called from childhood) was, in July 1941, awarded the

Squadron Leader Dennis Lockhart Armitage , DFC

Distinguished Flying Cross for his service not only to his country but also to the 266 Squadron. He was promoted to Squadron Leader of 129 Squadron in June 1941. It was while flying as Spitfire wing escort to the bombers on a mission over France in September 1941 that he was shot down, but managed to bale out safely. He was captured and imprisoned by the Germans and found that a fellow prisoner was the legendary Douglas Bader. They found themselves incarcerated in Poland and before Bader was transferred to Colditz the two men worked on a story of life in a prisoner of war camp. After the war was over they stayed in contact and tried to sell their idea of the play. They were immediately successful and after the play ran for a few weeks in London the BBC bought it from them in 1947.

Bill returned to Macclesfield after the war and found that he had to involve himself in the family textile spinning business and perhaps take it in a different direction. The firm, which was based in Bolton, necessitating a daily journey as Bill diversified into the carpet industry. In 1947 Bill met his wife to be Margaret, a Disley girl, and after a whirlwind courtship they married in October 1947 and set up home in Prestbury. However, despite running the family business in Bolton and being recently wed, Bill still retained his love and fascination for planes and was instrumental in helping to establish and run the Lancashire Aeronautical Club at the Barton Aerodrome.

After 25 years in Prestbury they moved to Rushton Spencer and after 12 years out in the countryside, with their sons and daughter departed, they moved to the tiny village of East Meon in Hampshire.

Squadron Leader Dennis (Bill) Lockhart Armitage DFC, British Spitfire fighter pilot, veteran of the Battle of Britain died on 3rd March, 2004 aged 92 in East Meon and is survived by his wife Margaret, two sons and a daughter.

Sergeant Dougie Wright MM

If all his alleged exploits are true then Sergeant Dougie Wright was Macclesfield's own James Bond. Indeed, following his death on 22nd February, 2008, his life and deeds were deemed sufficient enough to warrant his generous obituary in *The Daily Telegraph.*

Born on 11th March, 1919 in the sub district of Prestbury, he lived his early life in Poynton with Worth, technically in the Prestbury sub division. His father was a journeyman butcher and with a large family of nine children it was a struggle to make ends meet. As a youth the young Douglas worked as a baker's assistant and had a spell as a butcher's boy before working as a farmhand. Perhaps influenced by his father, who had served in the First World War with the Pioneer Corps, in 1938 Dougie enlisted in the Grenadier Guards at the age of 19. He was posted into the King's Company who must have presented a fearsome front to any enemy, as no man was under 6ft 3in tall.

It wasn't too long before he experienced real action as the Second World War commenced in 1939 and he was part of the force during the Dunkirk retreat. His obituary revealed the amusing story of the Grenadiers, under heavy fire, marching inexplicably in an orderly fashion. It was only when the order 'eyes right' was given and General Alexander acknowledged their salutes that they realised the reason for the formality. Dougie went on, "then some silly bugger forgot to give the halt, so we ended up in a foot of water".

His thirst for action and adventure resulted in him joining the SAS. After fighting in North Africa he found his niche when he joined the SBS (Special Boat Squadron).

He was fearless and took part in highly dangerous operations in raids on Sardinia, Crete, Yugoslavia and the Greek Islands. The very nature of the operations meant contact with the enemy was often at close quarters and hand-to-hand fighting was often unavoidable. It also meant that attacks had to be ruthless to protect the secrecy and the safety of fellow commandos.

Legend has it, although there is no positive evidence to support the story, that Wright strangled nine Germans during an operation in the Greek Islands.

However, what is fact is that during raids in April 1944 in the Greek Islands his group wiped out an enemy post on Ios and followed that with an attack on a radio station on Amorgos. The first attack was successful and Wright's leader agreed a deal with the wireless operator to save him in exchange for the station's codebooks and his dog. Dougie Wright took the German's mistress. It was later necessary to return and once again remove the threat at Amorgos but this time the Germans had reinforced and were waiting for them. It was Wright's job to provide the attack with cover from his Bren gun. He was positioned on a rooftop and at the signal to attack he opened fire as his colleagues moved into action. His accuracy was devastating and he killed six immediately as they ran for cover and five more during the resultant fighting.

The citation stated that the success of the attack was largely down to his efforts. He was not done yet and during further operations on Naxos from 16-26th May, when he was suffering from malaria, he refused to be a burden to his colleagues and carried his heavy equipment over the mountains on a journey of some fifteen miles.

For his bravery and determination Sergeant Douglas Wright was awarded the Military Medal.

This brave and fearless man was almost brought down by malaria and at the end of the war retired from the army. Unsurprisingly, unable to settle into a normal civilian life he re-enlisted in the Grenadiers and served for a time in Malta and then Cyprus.

He was unquestionably a tough man and told the story of being attacked by a guard dog that went for his throat, "having worked with farm animals, I wasn't having that so I bit the bastard back". The dog, so the story goes, beat a hasty retreat.

In London he had an altercation with a senior officer and lost his Long Service and Good Conduct Medal. Driven once more by the need for action he served in the Cameroons in Germany and Sharjah before finally, in 1970, leaving the army after 21 years of service.

He tried once again to settle into civilian life and had jobs with a butcher and a security firm before joining the prison service.

His way of life and his experiences must have made it difficult for an orderly and settled domestic life and both his marriages ended in divorce, although he had three children from each of his marriages. He eventually went to live in the Royal Hospital, Chelsea for army pensioners. Sadly his obituary recorded that in his room at the hospital his only possession was a bayonet that he had carried at Dunkirk and which had pride of place on the wall above his bunk; there were no family photographs.

Typical, it seems of the man, was a story that one day the Chelsea army pensioners were telling each other about their army exploits and stating how many of the enemy they had killed when Wright interjected with the bland statement, "sank a troopship once".

Sergeant Dougie Wright MM died on 27th February, 2008. He was a giant of his time.

Group Captain Zebulon Lewis Leigh, OBE, CM, ED

'Lewie' Leigh, as he was known was born in Macclesfield and emigrated to Canada as a toddler, where he became a Canadian hero and is entered in the Canadian Aviation Hall of Fame. Born on 19th June, 1906 to father Lewis a joiner and mother Sarah formerly Rowbotham, young Zebulon started his life at 60 Brook Street, Macclesfield but when he was a toddler the family moved to Alberta, Canada to start a new life. As a young man he became fascinated with aircraft and at a very early age began to learn to fly. At the age of 21 he became a flying instructor for Southern Alberta Airlines but he had ambitions and in 1929 started his own flying school operating out of Medicine Hat, Alberta. After two years of frustration he terminated the business and accepted the post of Chief Pilot for Maritime and Newfoundland Airways in Sydney, Nova Scotia with responsibility for Newfoundland and the Gulf of the St Lawrence.

One of his first tasks was to find a Heinkel seaplane that had been launched from the German ship Bremen. Leigh found the wreck and although he managed to extract the pilot he unfortunately later died from exposure. In 1932 Leigh undertook an instrument flying course with the Royal Canadian Air Force and then joined the Explorer's Air Transport of Sydney, still in Nova Scotia as Chief Pilot. However this appointment did not last and he became, briefly, an instructor at a flying club in Manitoba before joining Canadian Airways Ltd at Edmonton in 1934. His 'patch' was the Barren Lands and the Mackenzie River, a vast unsettled part of the Northwest Territories. He had his first taste of fame when his skills were required to track down a wanted killer who was on the run in this vast hostile territory. Leigh located and captured the man earning praise from the Royal Canadian Mounted Police for his skills.

In January 1936 Leigh was sent by Canadian Airways to the Boeing School of Aeronautics in Oakland, California on an advanced course of instrument, navigation and airline operations. Once qualified, he became Canada's first instrument-rated airline pilot and was put in charge of the Airways training school. He quickly became bored with teaching and lusted for action and in 1937 was employed as one of the first pilots for Trans-Canada Airlines and on 2nd April, 1939 flew the very first TCA westbound flight from Winnipeg, Manitoba to Vancouver, British Columbia.

However, the outbreak of the Second World War saw him restless for action and he resigned from TCA to join, as a Flight Lieutenant, the Royal Canadian Air Force patrolling the east coast. He was put in charge of the Operational Training Squadron at Patricia Bay, British Columbia before promotion in June 1942 to Wing Commander at Air Force Head Quarters in Ottawa, Ontario charged with organising Air Transport Command for the RCAF. The task was to link all Canadian military establishments, one aspect of which was to organise and operate a regular military mail service across the Atlantic to the UK, Italy and to North Africa. It was a daunting task and eventually embraced 688 flights across the Atlantic. Leigh's efforts were recognised and he was promoted to Group Captain.

Always a man of action he personally flew with the first transport aircraft into Normandy after the D-Day landings in June 1944, having previously been instrumental in organising the airlift of the very many casualties following the invasion. I wonder if any fellow Maxonians were among the wounded that he saved at Normandy?

He was rewarded in 1944 with the Officer of the Order of the British Empire (OBE) for his military services and after the war received from Canada the Efficiency Decoration (ED).

After the war when Field Marshall Montgomery of Alamein, the much acclaimed war hero, visited Canada Leigh was appointed air commander of the tour ensuring that the visit went smoothly to plan. However, the action man in Leigh elicited the post of commander of the Royal Canadian Air Force base at Goose Bay, Labrador giving him the opportunity to become involved in rescue missions. Yet another honour came his way when he was awarded the TransCanada McKee Trophy for 1946 for outstanding contributions to Canada air operations.

He was involved in rescue operations during the terrible Fraser River floods in the spring of 1948 and also in 1948 he was in control of a search and rescue operation trying to find an aircraft that went missing over northern Manitoba. It was akin to searching for a needle in a haystack but after thirteen days the crew, which included the British and American Naval Attaches, were found and rescued; Leigh received the United States Legion of Merit.

In 1950 he was posted to Ottawa as Director of Air Operations for the Royal Canadian Air Force. Before retiring in 1957, as Commander of No 2 Air Defence Group in Toronto, he served in several capacities including planning a Korean airlift from Canada to Japan.

In retirement he served for almost ten years as the Director of Operations of the Canadian National Exhibition Air Show before relinquishing the post in 1966. In 1974 he received the accolade of being inducted into Canada's Aviation Hall of Fame and in 1989 received the ultimate award from his adopted country, the CM, the Order of Canada.

Zebulon Lewis Leigh, a Macclesfield lad, who crossed the Atlantic to find fortune and fame and become a hero of his adopted country, died at Grimsby, Ontario on 22nd December, 1996.

Explorers

Sir Philip Lee Brocklehurst – Explorer and Soldier
It is almost impossible to write about Macclesfield without mentioning the all powerful and influential Brocklehurst family. It was in 1745 when John Brocklehurst joined Acton Street button makers in Hurdsfield Road and later helped expand the business into silk

throwing becoming, with Charles Roe, the pivotal influence in establishing Macclesfield, as not only the leading producer of silk in the UK but also very prominent in the world market. Indeed Brocklehurst and Whiston, silk manufacturers continued trading until 1992.

The Brocklehursts have featured virtually in every aspect of Macclesfield's social and cultural history. At various times, seven in total, a Brocklehurst was appointed mayor of the town, they owned one of the first banks, supplied the first powered fire engine, became the largest land owner and employer and held a whole host of local appointments including President of the Macclesfield Silk Managers Association and started, and held, the first appointment as President of Macclesfield Chamber of Commerce.

However, on the national scene another John Brocklehurst became Member of Parliament for Macclesfield after the town's first ever parliamentary election in 1832, serving the town with great distinction for more than 30 years. He was a kind and generous man and was a champion of the town's working class people. During the hard times he was personally generous and was vociferous in their support in the House of Commons. His son William Coare Brocklehurst succeeded him as MP and in 1908 Colonel WB Brocklehurst continued the family tradition when also elected MP for the town.

In 1894, Frances Dicken Brocklehurst JP gave Macclesfield Victoria Park and in 1896 Marianne Brocklehurst gave the town the West Park Museum.

At various times, over the generations, the families have lived in Hurdsfield House, Fence House, Pear Tree Cottage now Jordangate House, Henbury, Tytherington and indeed my former house Brocklebank, Beech Lane, Macclesfield.

Unquestionably the family's wealth gave them opportunities denied to the majority of the population and several of them indulged in foreign travel and exploration.

Marianne Brocklehurst, born in 1832, lived most of her life in Wincle and in her later years became an intrepid traveller. For more than 30 years from 1860 to 1892 she travelled the world when it was a dangerous and unstable place, particularly for a woman. Her travels took her through Europe to the Middle East embracing Syria, Jordan, Saudi Arabia, Israel and Egypt, volatile dangerous parts of the world with scant regard for the safety of women.

Her lady friend, Miss Booth accompanied her, as did her liveried footman. She kept a diary of her travels and illustrated it with watercolour sketches. In 1873 after a four-month journey down the Nile collecting antiquities, hunting crocodiles and smuggling artefacts she returned to Macclesfield and dedicated her treasures, including the diary and a mummy case, to the new West Park Museum which she created and opened in 1896.

Thomas Unett Brocklehurst, who resided at Henbury Hall, travelled extensively from 1879-82 in America, Japan and Mexico and is credited infamously with introducing the grey squirrel to this country. The creature is now regarded as vermin and is now overrunning the countryside. Frances Dicken Brocklehurst of Fence Avenue, Macclesfield spent three years, 1858-61 travelling in the Far East and very daringly travelling often disguised as a man, through Tibet.

However the most renowned of the family for his exploration activities was Sir Philip Lee Brocklehurst. He was a descendant of John Brocklehurst, of Hurdsfield, Macclesfield's first MP in 1832, who in 1831 bought Swythamley Hall. John Brocklehurst's son Philip Lancaster Brocklehurst was born at Swythamley and later became a Baronet and the father of Sir Philip Lee Brocklehurst.

Although Philip Lee Brocklehurst was born at Swythamley Park in Staffordshire he is from a long well established Macclesfield family and therefore merits our attention.

Born on 7th March, 1887 into wealth and privilege he became a baronet in 1903 at the age of 16. He was an adventurous young man educated at Eton and then while at Trinity Hall, Cambridge University, 1906 he became a boxing blue. It was also at Cambridge where he met the man, Ernest Henry Shackleton, who would define his later years. Indeed within a year and at the age of 20, in 1907, Philip was invited to join Shackleton's British Antarctic Expedition. Shackleton had been part of the tragic Captain Robert Scott's first expedition into the 'lost continent' Antarctica in 1902 but during the latter stages in 1903 he had been ordered home by Scott because of his failing health. He was determined to return to Antarctica and continue the search for the elusive South Pole.

Records indicate that the young Brocklehurst was taken on the expedition as a scientific assistant but another states that his function was that of assistant geologist. No doubt the young man would have served and welcomed the invitation to embark on such a fantastic opportunity at whatever level.

The serious part of the expedition commenced when the party sailed from New Zealand on 1st January, 1908, heading south in the small vessel, the Nimrod. Shackleton was surprised at the reduction in ice from his last visit to the Ross Shelf and soon found himself in danger in the increased waters and prevailing winds blowing the ship onto the ice-shelf. The party safely made it to McMurdo Sound and set up base camp close to Ross Island, in order to lay the eventual chain of supply depots as far across the ice as possible to enable the eventual four man strike party to travel with the minimum amount of weight towards the South Pole. The breaking ice delayed preparations for almost a year. In the meantime Philip Brocklehurst and his colleagues were able to conduct research and geologically map the area in greater detail.

In October Shackleton, along with three companions and four ponies, set off on foot to travel 1750 miles across the barren frozen wastes into the unknown and back in search of the South Pole. The journey was horrendously tough and they were just 97 miles short of the Pole when their last pony fell into an ice crevasse. The four men were dangerously ill from starvation and frostbite and were forced to abort the mission and return but 30 miles from safety they ran out of food. Shackleton feared that the end was in sight and recorded in his diary that they were all close to death. Although they had not achieved their objective to be the first to reach the South Pole – they had beaten Captain Scott's first expedition by 366 miles – they had travelled further south than any other expedition, had discovered the magnetic South Pole and found the route to the South Pole over the Beardmore Glacier.

While the strike party was away the rest of the team, including the young Brocklehurst, conducted explorations of the surrounding territory. His team were the first to ascend the volcanic mountain Mount Erebus but sadly frost bitten feet prevented him from achieving the ascent. Despite the amputation of toes he participated in several expeditions exploring the Taylor Valley and traversing the Ferrar Glacier. Shackleton, who was knighted on his return, returned to Antarctica again in 1914. The young Brocklehurst would not, although he would go on to greater achievements. However, he did attain lasting fame from his participation, however modest, in Shackleton's expedition. His conscientious participation in the expedition earned him a much-coveted Royal Geographical Society medal in 1909.

An indication of how well regarded Brocklehurst was by Sir Ernest Shackleton was evidenced in the fact that when Brocklehurst, in 1913, married Gladys Murray, Shackleton was his best man.

In the Macclesfield village of Wincle the pub sign of the Ship Inn is a painting of the Nimrod battling through the ice. The landlord Leslie Wright, a close friend of Philip Brocklehurst, was given a two-inch refracting telescope in a military case, which Brocklehurst had used in the Antarctic. Years later Sir Philip Brocklehurst moved from Swythamley Hall and moved into Wincle village. Bizarrely, in 2000, Christie's, London, sold at auction a biscuit from the Antarctic expedition belonging to Brocklehurst from which he had taken a bite, for the princely sum of £4,935!

Shortly after returning from Antarctica, Brocklehurst commenced a career in the military. During his time at Cambridge he was also commissioned in the Derbyshire Yeomanry and at the outbreak of the First World War he fought with the First Life Guards from 1914-17. He was wounded for his bravery and awarded the DSO. At the end of the war he served with the Egyptian Army until 1920. In 1920 he was knighted and in 1924 was made a brevet Lieutenant Colonel. He also travelled the world indulging in his love of exploration and big game hunting.

Giant Panda, West Park Museum, Macclesfield

However, once again, duty called and during the Second World War he commanded the Second Regiment of the Arab Legion, the Desert Mechanised Brigade and from 1943-44 he served with the British Council in Palestine-Trans Jordan. Finally, at the end of the war in 1945, he returned to Macclesfield and to his family estate at Swythamley.

Perhaps because of his thirst for adventure and the need for action in his life his marriage suffered and in 1947 he was divorced. When he died on 28th January, 1975 he was the last survivor of Shackleton's Antarctic Expedition of 1907-09.

When his estate was being sold in May 1976 there was a huge auction, held at the hall, of artefacts and big-game trophies collected from around the world that attracted collectors from all over the world including myself. There was a vast array of big-game trophies from elephant, buffalo, lion, leopard, walrus, snakes and many other species from the Arctic, the Antarctic, India, Africa, Newfoundland and the Sudan. I bought, much to my wife's disgust a crocodile head that had been shot in Tanganyika and later mounted on a wooden shield and a lion's head!

In the Brocklehurst's heyday big-game hunting was a way of life, a hobby, and a plaything for the wealthy. His brother, Lieutenant Colonel Henry Courtney Brocklehurst, was at one time the game warden of the Sudan and was also a professional big-game hunter as well as an explorer. He earned a considerable amount of infamy when in China, in 1935, he shot a giant panda believed to have been one of the biggest ever seen. He had it stuffed and resisted an attempt by Hermann Goering to buy it off him during the Berlin Exhibition, just before the start of the Second World War. The panda can be seen in Macclesfield's West Park Museum.

Benedict Allen

For many of us the old stories of British explorers trekking through dense jungle, fighting off wild animals and fierce looking natives before coming finally to a jungle clearing and finding a fabled 'Lost City' glittering with gold, have fuelled our imaginations over generations. In today's modern world of high tech satellite probes and navigation systems one would think that there was little left to explore and that the art of exploration had gone forever. You would be wrong. Macclesfield has produced its very own Doctor Livingstone, a modern day Indianna Jones, Benedict Allen.

Born in Macclesfield in 1961, Benedict was brought up in Prestbury at Foxholes, Chalfont Lane to be precise, with his two older siblings. Mum was a busy housewife and mother while dad was a test pilot based at Woodford, just down the road. Benedict told me that he has a vivid memory of his father flying Vulcan bombers over their house! He remembers going to school in Prestbury, the stocks in the middle of the village, a Punch and Judy show and walking over the golf course in the snow. He recalls wonderful days of going to Manchester Airport to see the planes, little knowing of course that one day he would be using them to fly all round the world.

The family left the area when he was seven as his father had a job offer at Heathrow. Although his mother, who had supported and worried over him over the years as his adventures abroad became more and more dangerous, died in 1994 and his father in 2006. Benedict says that he still comes back to this area from time to time to visit friends and relatives. The very popular watering hole the Bridge Hotel, Prestbury has named its restaurant after the village's favourite son, Benedict's.

Allen's adventures have been recorded in a series of books and in several BBC television documentaries and it is estimated that he has escaped death on at least six occasions. He took several jobs, including a spell in a warehouse, in order to save the money for his first big trip.

His very first escapade, at the age of 22 in 1983, was a 600-mile trek through parts of the Amazon jungle on foot and by river. He survived malaria, an attempt to murder him by gold prospectors and, after his guides had deserted him and his canoe capsized, he was taken ill and faced with starvation. In true explorer tradition he sadly had to kill and eat his only companion, his dog.

On a further expedition to the Amazon the local Indians called the 6ft 4in tall visitor, 'Mad White Giant' but he earned their respect by not only witnessing some of their more harrowing rituals but also by taking part! In Colombia drug runners tried to kill him and in New Guinea he actually made the highly dangerous first contact with two 'lost' tribes; two unknown tribes who had never experienced contact with the outside world, let alone encountered a giant 'white' man. He gained their trust and respect and spent weeks living with them observing and complying with their ways and their hospitality; one of their rituals was a daily beating! In order to prove that he was as strong as a crocodile he endured a daily ritual of scarification with sharp instruments until he bled and he still has the scars that proved his endurance.

What is unique about Benedict Allen is his refusal to take with him a film crew, insisting "It's important just to immerse yourself, and go on their terms" (i.e. the local people). He has from the outset filmed his own travels.

Television viewers must have watched in awe as the documentary of his trip to Sumatra in search of the ape- man was aired. Allen split his chest open on a piece of bamboo and without any assistance managed to stitch up the gash in his chest with a boot-mending kit!

In Siberia he once again had a lucky escape when, during the 1000-mile trek being pulled along the frozen wastes by a dog sled, the dogs in their enthusiasm catapulted the sledge over a cliff; miraculously they all survived. The five-month trip had started in Mongolia venturing through parts of Siberia down through the steppes and finishing with a 100-mile trek through the Gobi Desert.

Benedict Allen in the Amazon (courtesy of Catherine Marsh)

He crossed Australia's notorious Gibson Desert and spent more than four months crossing the dangerous Namib Desert by camel. Nevertheless there was more to come. In 1999 he went in pursuit of the explorer Colonel Percy Fawcett who, along with his expedition, disappeared in the jungles of Brazil in 1925, never to be seen again. It was riveting stuff and came close to solving the mystery with several native witnesses suggesting where and when Fawcett had been murdered.

Allen once again had another lucky escape in Siberia in 2001. His mission was to cross the frozen Bering Strait and the trip was enthralling edge of the seat stuff. There was a breathtaking moment when Allen foolishly left his dogs and sled to scout ahead and when he returned they had all gone. He was left standing alone in that vast, empty, white, sparse landscape in temperatures of –40'C, defenceless and vulnerable. He tried to light his stove but it didn't respond and his only course of action was to curl up for warmth and hope that he could survive the night and hope that the dogs would return at daylight. Once again the fates smiled on him and when he woke at daybreak the dogs had returned. If they had not it would have meant certain death.

There is evidence though that our intrepid explorer is slowing down. Benedict Allen is now married to Lenka from Czechoslovakia, a 26 year old whom he met when she came to this country to learn our language and they now have a nine-month-old little girl. He has spent a lifetime travelling with great freedom around the world with no responsibilities. That in itself made relationships extremely difficult. After all, who wants to wait for six months every now and again while your mate clears off round the world. When questioned in a national newspaper interview in July 2008 whether this uncertainty had caused his relationship with the Texan model Jerry Hall, ex wife of Mick Jagger, to terminate, Benedict refused to be drawn.

He did confess though that although there were several places in the world still tempting him, Papua New Guinea, parts of the Amazon and a trek across the world's most barren and waterless desert, China's Takla Makan he has lately, at the age of 48, come to feel mortal and has developed a fear of dying. His explorations no longer seem to be a game and he marvels at how he has survived. He has responsibilities and doesn't want his young wife and daughter spending years worrying about him like his mother did.

These days part of his time is spent giving motivational talks and after dinner speeches and when he gets the time he visits schools to give talks on his travels.

Benedict Allen is a real throw back; he has lived the dream that many of us have nurtured from the warmth and safety of our armchair. On a cold winters night clutching a whiskey or glass of wine watching his exploits on the screen, "I could have done that". Oh no you couldn't!! His exploits have brought us pleasure, knowledge and a real feel for the wonders of our planet.

The Music Business

Macclesfield has an outstanding record of producing people who have excelled in the complex, demanding and highly competitive world of the music business. The town can boast eminently respected musicians, top selling pop groups, disc jockeys, one of whom allegedly started the whole business of promoting popular music and instigated the phrase, 'flower power' that for a time dominated the pop music crazy era of the 1960s, and one of Britain's finest opera singers.

Ian Curtis – Lead Singer in Joy Division

Unquestionably Macclesfield's most famous group Joy Division achieved national fame, a best selling record *Love Will Tear Us Apart*, a record contract, a large following and an American tour establishing them amongst the very best. However, the suicide of their charismatic but troubled lead singer Ian Curtis, in 1980, just before the start of the tour ended their attack on the American market.

After his death the group reformed as New Order but never achieved the levels of Joy Division. In 2007 interest in the life of Ian Curtis and the group was rekindled when a film of his life, *Control*, was released to much acclaim and was followed by a much praised documentary film, *Joy Division*, in 2008.

Ian Kevin Curtis was born in Manchester on 15th July, 1956 but moved to Macclesfield as a baby. The family, Ian had a sister Carole, lived in Hurdsfield Road and Ian's first school was Trinity Square Primary School. He showed an early interest in writing and drawing perhaps inherited from his father who, although he was in the Transport Commission Police, was an unpublished writer, mainly of plays.

The family house was demolished and they were moved into the new controversial Victoria Flats development in 1965. At the age of 10 Ian formed his first band from his pals who used to go caddying with him at Prestbury Golf Club. Ian did well at Hurdsfield Junior School and passed his 11 plus examinations and qualified for the King's School. At the time this was quite an achievement; a lad from the soon to be notorious 'Vicky Flats' qualifying for the grammar school, arguably the best in the north of England.

However, he found it hard at King's School, the affluence, the discipline and the demanding standards, but he had a hard core of friends some of whom were from more affluent families. He was also disliked mainly because he was different: he enjoyed shocking people with his often outrageous clothes and his black nail varnish. He was very much an acquired taste. He had a passion for music and would go home at lunch-time with friends to listen and play. Even then he was a controversial character and would steal records from stalls in the indoor market and alcohol from off-licenses; he started to inhale insolvents, and smoked dope. King's School had a community programme ensuring that pupils visited the elderly and the needy taking them to bingo or running errands. Ian and his pals would search the old peoples houses for drugs and many an afternoon was spent in Sparrow Park inhaling cleaning fluids and popping pills. During this time fellow pupil Stephen Morris, a year younger than Ian, was expelled from King's School for the abusive use of cough medicine – but more about him later.

In her moving book about her husband, *Touching From a Distance*, Deborah Curtis was very honest in mentioning Ian's characteristics which with the great gift of hindsight might have prevented the tragedy that later would envelop him.

At times he was weird with an apparent obsession with death, particularly dead celebrities, and he often said that he would not live beyond the age of 25. He had a preoccupation with pain and would inflict injuries on himself in order to see how much he could stand. He passed out on several occasions and friends attributed it to drugs but perhaps it was the first sign of the epilepsy that was later diagnosed and perhaps if it had been treated successfully would have eased his frequent bouts of depression. Nevertheless he was regarded by many as odd and by a few as charismatic, including a young Macclesfield High School girl who would go on to make a national name for herself as an actress, Helen Atkinson Wood.

In December 1972 Ian asked Deborah Woodruff, another Macclesfield High School girl to go to a David Bowie gig with him. As their relationship developed he became more controlling and flew into jealous tantrums and on more than one occasion he told her that he had no intention of living beyond his mid twenties!

In the spring of 1973 the Curtis family left Macclesfield to return to Manchester and Ian went with them leaving King's School for good, with, despite all that had passed a highly commendable 7 'O' levels.

For a time he sought employment, including a job with Jonathan King in London, but eventually settled for a post with Rare Records in Manchester while Debbie worked as a clerk at ICI in Macclesfield. His moods she recalled still fluctuated wildly from warm and generous to cold, arrogant and possessive. However when she tried to end the relationship he would become distraught. Nevertheless despite the doubts from her family, they became engaged in April 1974. Ian worked with the Ministry of Defence in Cheadle Hulme and later with Manpower Services in Piccadilly Gardens, Manchester. They married on 23rd August, 1975 at St Thomas's Church, Henbury with the reception at the Bulls Head in the market place in Macclesfield, followed by a honeymoon in Paris.

For a time they lived with relatives before eventually returning to Macclesfield and 77 Barton Street in May 1977.

Inspired by the Sex Pistols in 1976, Ian heard that old school pals from their Salford Grammar School days, Peter Hook, Bernard Sumner and Terry Mason had formed a band but needed a singer. He asked if he could join them (he couldn't play an instrument); they called themselves Warsaw. For a time they played pub gigs and Ian infamously one night deliberately gashed his leg on stage with a broken bottle.

When the band needed a new drummer Ian placed an advert in Jones's Music Shop, Victoria Street, Macclesfield. Former pupil Stephan Morris who had been expelled from King's School applied for the job and got it. Ian was now calling the shots and under his influence the group changed its name and Joy Division was born. However they still had day jobs and Ian was transferred, luckily, to the Employment Exchange at South Park Road, Macclesfield as an Assistant Disablement Resettlement Officer, where he proved to be a good and conscientious employee. During this time he went on an epilepsy course and managed to get the influential producer Tony Wilson to promote a television campaign about the condition.

Ian was now driving the band and after obtaining a bank loan for 'household effects' he used the money to produce their first record, *An Ideal For Living*. A home spun affair, recorded in Oldham in December 1977; Bernard Sumner designed the sleeve, Steve Morris arranged the printing in Macclesfield and folding the posters and packing the records was done in Steve Morris's house in Macclesfield.

Warsaw played its last gig on New Years Eve 1977 and Joy Division played its first gig at Pips Disco, Manchester on 25th January, 1978.

In the meantime the band continued with their day jobs and it was a strenuous time. Competition was extremely tough and Ian was aggressive in his pursuit of publicity, hounding Tony Wilson into getting television air-time – so essential for a new band. They appeared on *What's On* and were invited back to film *Transmission* and *She's Lost Control.*

In the autumn of 1978 Deborah was pregnant and during a London gig Ian had his first acknowledged epileptic attack and was hospitalised; the attacks became more frequent – sometimes three a week.

In January 1979 he appeared on the front cover of the *New Musical Express.* It was an iconic shot of him dressed in a long green coat, a quizzical, half sneer on his face with a cigarette poised between his lips. He and the band had arrived and towards the end of January they appeared on the *John Peel Show.*

Nevertheless, despite this success the lads still had full time jobs. Ian's health had deteriorated and towards the end of January he was prescribed drugs to control his epilepsy. However the drugs also had the effect of promoting depression and his mood swings were quite marked from happy to morose, from conciliatory to violent and it was often Deborah who bore the brunt.

He managed to hold his day job whilst at the same time writing lyrics that were often depressing and seeking to promote the group.

On 16th April, 1979 his daughter, Natalie was born. Also in April Joy Division produced their first album, *Unknown Pleasures*, recorded at Strawberry Studios, Stockport and paid for by Tony Wilson. It should have been a wonderful milestone year in his life but ill health dogged him and in May he collapsed and was taken to hospital. He recovered but was so sensitive that he became jealous of the attention Deborah was giving to their baby. He was juggling perhaps too much for his fragile state of health: day job, band, and home life.

Joy Division started their own publishing company with each member of the band taking 20%,with manager Rob Gretton also taking 20%, despite the fact that it was Ian Curtis who wrote all the lyrics and the melodies. He didn't seem to mind the inequality but resented the media referring to the band as Ian Curtis and Joy Division – he was not such an egotist.

Unknown Pleasures was released in June 1979 and, perhaps with the portend of what was to come, one critic said that the tracks were ideal for someone contemplating suicide! Fame was beckoning but for

Deborah their home life was unpredictable. She could not understand why he had married and had a child if he was determined to kill himself, it just didn't make sense. There were long periods of silence at home and, although success was on the way, travel away from home and his fragile state of health did not improve his quality of life.

On the road he had an affair with Annik Honore, a Belgian girl, which caused problems in the band, while back home Deborah had to work hard to make ends meet. Ian told her that he couldn't afford to take her on the road but he paid for Annik to accompany him. Furthermore he told Deborah that she couldn't tour America with the band. Eventually Ian admitted to the affair and promised to end it, but didn't. He was torn between two women. In March 1980 Joy Division recorded *Closer* in London and in April Ian suffered severe epileptic attacks on stage and later took an overdose.

It was Tony Wilson who comforted Deborah as Ian recovered and later in April the band resumed their tour of Britain. Deborah went to see them at one gig where the wives told her that they had had a great time in London while the band recorded *Closer* and that all the band and wives shared rooms but Ian had one to himself with Annik; Deborah was heartbroken. Later on 25th April, 1980 Joy Division recorded the song that would forever be linked with them and the one which set them on the world stage, *Love Will Tear Us Apart.*

However their private life was nothing short of disastrous and Ian agreed to see a psychiatrist at Parkside, ironically where Deborah had once worked, in order to understand his attempted suicide.

April and May were busy as the band were much in demand and when Deborah discovered that Ian was staying with Annik she snapped and told him that she wanted a divorce. Ian responded by telling her that he would never come home to her. She was upset because she also believed that far from being back on the road he should have been in hospital receiving treatment knowing that a big American tour was in the offing.

Unbeknown to everyone Ian Curtis and Joy Division played what was to be their last gig together at Birmingham University on 2nd May, 1980.

Days later Ian apparently was in good form. He had visited the epilepsy clinic and appeared to be getting his life together, although friends said later that he was acting strangely and was giving personal things away. He was living with his parents and hadn't seen Deborah in weeks . Also he had had no epileptic fits for several weeks.

On Tuesday 13th May he came to Macclesfield to visit Deborah and his daughter Natalie at Barton Street and brought fresh flowers and had a picture taken with Natalie. Deborah thought that that would be the last time she saw him before the band's big trip to the USA and they parted amicably.

Peter Hook saw him on the Friday and remembered how excited they were at the thought of jetting off to the States in a couple of days and they agreed to get together on Saturday. Ian rang him later and told him that he couldn't make it as he had promised to go and see Deborah. He told manager Rob Gretton that he was going to watch a film in private about a man who kills himself because he is in love with two women and can't choose between them.

Despite all the signs the band still had no idea what was to come and could never understand why they missed the tell-tale signs. Bernard Sumner said that he was sure that Ian wasn't worried about the American trip, and Stephan Morris later said that if he was depressed about going he hid it very successfully from them. However, Deborah's view was quite succinct; she said that Ian was terrified of flying, was worried about the USA attitude to his epilepsy and the reason that he didn't appear worried about the USA trip to his band members was simply because, "he knew he wasn't going". He had talked so often about suicide that quite clearly, if he was going to do it, this was the ideal time.

He asked to see Deborah on Saturday but as she was working as a barmaid, despite his credentials as a rock star about to jet off to America, she told him she would be home later and to let himself in. When she arrived he had watched the film and, in a rambling conversation, asked her to stop the divorce but continued to talk about Annik. He agreed to the concerned Deborah's offer to stay the night and return later to Barton Street. When she returned in the early hours Ian had again changed his mind and asked her to leave and not to return to the house until after 10am the following morning by which time he promised he would be gone. Sometime in the early morning he commenced to write a letter telling Deborah of his love for her and for Natalie, saying how much he hated Annik admitting that he was unable to tell her to her face. He also mentioned that he wished he was dead but made no express threat.

As requested, Deborah and Natalie returned to Barton Street after 10am the following morning: there was a light on, the curtains were closed and she noticed an envelope on the mantelpiece. Then she turned slightly and saw him apparently kneeling in the kitchen, a rope from the clothes rack tightly around his neck. His destiny appeared to have been fulfilled, he killed himself at the age of 23 with the world about to be laid at his feet.

Ian Curtis's headstone, Macclesfield Cemetry

It was Deborah Curtis who designed the memorial kerbstone in the Macclesfield Cemetery, which is visited by fans from around the world with the Americans and Japanese being most in attendance. The inscription states 'Ian Curtis, 18-5-80' with the words 'Love Will Tear Us Apart'.

The three remaining members of the band went on to form a new band, New Order.

Stephen Morris – Joy Division and New Order

Although Ian Curtis, as front man and lyricist, commanded the headlines the three other members of the band were highly accomplished musicians in their own right.

Fellow Maxonian Stephen Morris is still performing today almost thirty years after Curtis's death. Ostensibly his early career was as a drummer but he also plays keyboards and sometimes performs as a vocalist.

Born in Macclesfield on 28th October, 1957, Steve grew up on Gawsworth Road, Macclesfield with sister Amanda and mother and father Clifford and Hilda Morris. Stephen was educated at Christ Church Primary School, which sadly no longer exists and proved that he was an intelligent youngster when passing his 11 plus and qualifying for the King's School.

In 2008 Steve gave an interview to the *Macclesfield Express* in which he recalled his earlier memories of the town. He loved locally made oatcakes and when attending his Grandma's house in Coronation Street he would be sent to the bakers in White Street to collect them. He loved to watch them being made and admitted that sometimes he would eat one before returning home. He recalled walking from Gawsworth road with his pals, crossing the fields or traversing Park Lane to get into town, the huge Christmas tree in the market place and the festive lights all the way up Chestergate. Even during the heady days of his music career he often returned to Macclesfield.

He admits that he was a rebellious kid and his education at King's School came to a rapid end when he was expelled for the abusive use of cough medicine. However, he was by now very much into music nurtured by his father's love of jazz but initially disappointed his father by neglecting his clarinet lessons to take up the drums.

During the day he would work in his father's kitchen manufacturing firm and he also worked in a textile mill but at night would practise on the drums.

His life changed when he answered the advert in Jones's Music Shop in Victoria Street, placed by Ian Curtis on behalf of the Warsaw group, seeking a drummer. The dye was cast. He was 20 and music was to be his life.

The band changed its name and was signed by Factory Records of Manchester but Steve still liked his home comforts and regularly returned home to his parents for meals and company.

One day Stephen and the band were practising at the same place as a young girls punk band and he recognised one of the girls, Gillian Gilbert, who had been featured on the front page of the *Macclesfield Express* in 1978 and offered her a lift home. They became an item and

Steve moved out of his parent's house into a terraced house in Hurdsfield Road with Gillian.

Joy Division were now achieving national acclaim and Steve admits that Ian Curtis's suicide was a shock as they were good friends and he believed that the band was really on the way up and set for global success. None of the band had realised just how troubled Ian had been.

However life has to continue and Joy Division manager Rob Gretton offered Gillian the spare place in the band to play keyboard and guitar and changed the name of the band to New Order.

New Order continued to do well issuing more than a dozen albums, videos and discs and were regularly in demand. Later Peter Hook left the band and was replaced by another Macclesfield lad Phil Cunningham.

Steve and Gillian formed a duo calling themselves The Other Two, before Gillian also left New Order to take care of her family; daughters Mathilde (Tilly) now 13 and Grace now 9, due to health reasons, require care and attention which had limited Gillian's ability to tour with the band.

Steve, now a 53 year old family man, is still very much attached to Macclesfield having spent the last 18 years living in Rainow and is very much a part of the village life. In the summer of 2008 he was a judge in the village's scarecrow competition and just enjoys the pace of country life.

He admitted to the *Macclesfield Express* that it was weird seeing films about himself. He mused that it was hard to believe that he had somehow been part of all that believing that things like that are usually shown after your death.

The wild days of touring and adulation have gone but Steve enjoys working in the quiet and calm of his own home.

New Order have not made a record since 2005 but he is content and busy, indeed he and Gillian had remixed two tracks for the *Nine Inch Nails* remix album *Year Zero Remixed*.

Phil Cunningham, Rock Musician – New Order

Born in Macclesfield on 17th December, 1974 Phil, a talented guitar and keyboard player, joined New Order as a replacement for Gillian Gilbert. He had joined the band as a session musician in 2001 and became a fully-fledged member in 2004. In 2008 New Order comprised of Bernard Sumner, Stephen Morris and Phil Cunningham.

During the 1990s he was a member of the pop group Marion and has recently reformed the band with a new lead singer Jaime Harding. His involvement with the Run Run Run band had to cease, contractually, when he joined New Order.

John Mayall – Legendary Blues Musician

Successful as they undoubtedly were, with loyal fans around the world, it cannot be said that Joy Division were the greatest or most successful musicians ever to come from Macclesfield. Many music fans across the spectrum would perhaps plump for Macclesfield's John Mayall. It was a matter of great satisfaction to me when a few years ago I was browsing through a record store in New York and came across a rack of John Mayall CDs and basked in the knowledge that he was a fellow Maxonian.

Our town has the most tenuous and yet the strongest of links to Mayall because, although he was born John Brumwell Mayall, in Macclesfield on 29th November, 1933, his parents lived in Cheadle Hulme where he was brought up. His father, Frederick Murray Hyde Mayall was described as being of independent means and his mother was Beryl Veronica Mayall, formerly Leeson.

His father, an enthusiastic amateur dance band musician keen on jazz with a comprehensive record collection, fostered his early interest in music and, before reaching his teens, John was playing guitar and learning to master the piano. His early interest was the blues and like his father he started to build an impressive record collection that would form the teaching foundation of his future band recruits.

However during his teens his intention was to become a commercial artist although whilst at art school he formed his first band, The Powerhouse Four. In 1961, encouraged by the success of his music, he changed the band's name to the Blues Syndicate and started to get professional engagements in the Manchester area, often appearing at the Twisted Wheel. He was persuaded to move to London where there was a more receptive market for the blues. On arrival in January 1963 he once again changed the name of his band to the Bluesbreakers, a name that would become synonymous with his later success and the many famous musicians who would later come under his wing.

It was a painstaking business recruiting the right type of musician to complement the music he wished to convey and there were many

John Mayall, father of British rhythm and blues (courtesy of Rod MacSween)

casualties. He signed a record deal with Decca in February 1964 and recorded *Crawling Up a Hill* and *Mr James*. In 1965 he released his first album *John Mayall Plays John Mayall*. Nevertheless, he was still seeking perfection in order to reproduce a Chicago style of blues and continued to seek fresh faces.

In April 1965, a man who would become one of the truly great iconic guitar players of his age, Eric Clapton, signed on with John Mayall after leaving the Yardbirds. For a time the band was hugely successful. John Mayall played keyboards and guitar and performed vocals, the rhythm section was John McVie on bass, Hughie Flint on drums and Eric Clapton starring on guitar. In 1966 they released a superb best selling album, *The Bluesbreakers Featuring Eric Clapton*, that proved to be the most important British blues album ever recorded and projected Clapton into a spotlight, which he never lost. Sadly by the time the album reached the top 10 best selling records in July 1966, Clapton and Jack Bruce had left Mayall to form the group Cream.

Undaunted Mayall recruited excellent guitarist Peter Green and in 1967 the album *Hard Road*, was acknowledged by the experts as being as good or if not better than the album produced with Clapton. Mayall had not lost his touch for recruitment and production or for hard work. In 1967 he recorded an album, *The Blues Alone*, for the Decca subsidiary Ace of Clubs for which he not only wrote the 12 tracks but also played all the instruments, except the drums, and completed the recording all on the same day! One of his favourite events was to link up and play with genuine American blues artists which he did on a number of occasions.

Personnel in his band continued to change, Mick Fleetwood who would later found the hugely successful group Fleetwood Mac with Peter Green stayed for a while before leaving with Green.

Mayall had the reputation, the expertise and the experience to attract a whole host of musicians to whatever project he was undertaking. American and British blues artists and others across the genre came under his influence. Many regard *Crusade* as the last strictly blues album that he made and *Bare Wires*, released in 1968, bore no relation to *Chicago Blues*, so Mayall's focus was changing and moving more toward jazz.

For a time he moved to Los Angeles and released *Blues from Laurel Canyon* having decided to drop the Bluesbreakers name. Shortly after, he left Decca and signed for Polydor Records making the album

Turning Point, recorded in New York in 1969 without a lead guitarist or drummer. He was seeking a new direction for his blues music.

He decided to become resident in Los Angeles and formed an American band that included several former members of Canned Heat. The music diversified with Mayall writing lyrics on political issues, drugs, police abuse and social deprivation typified by the album *USA Union*, released in 1970. The following ten years he worked prolifically both on tour and in the studio recording a number of albums that sadly were not altogether popular with his fans.

However in 1982, John McVie, despite enjoying huge success with Fleetwood Mac proposed a revival of the Bluesbreakers, which gave John Mayall the incentive he required to regenerate himself. The band, with new members including Walter Trout from Canned Heat as lead guitar after McVie had departed, once again went from strength to strength particularly in Europe. The experts regard albums released in 1990 and in 1993 when Mayall was 60 as being among his very best.

In his almost 50 years in the music business John Myall is universally regarded as being amongst the very best. He was a strong influence over Eric Clapton, who would later form Cream and gave him his first big break, Mick Fleetwood who later formed Fleetwood Mac and many other musicians several of whom went on to form their own groups. Over the years though the personnel in his bands changed they often returned to work on later projects with him, a true testimony of the regard that world-class musicians had for him. He had an unrivalled work ethic and typically, in 1999, at the age of 66 he performed at the Manchester Evening News Arena on 29th April as the support act to American legend BB King. However just as I was finishing this book I noticed that BB King was once again touring Britain and headlining with him was John Mayall, it was April 2009 and Mayall was 77!!

'Lord' Tim Hudson – DJ, Rock Star Manager, Entrepreneur

The popular music business probably started in the 1950s, then accelerated through the 1960s with the advent of 'flower power' and the Beatles. The popularity of the music and the artists led of course to immense record sales, the promotion of which spawned a whole new branch of show business; polished, witty, chat merchants promoted the records by playing them over the airways and this new genre of entertainers called themselves disc jockeys or DJs.

Macclesfield had its very own Tim Hudson or 'Lord' Tim Hudson as he was eventually known. But he was much more than a DJ, he was an opportunist and at various times a rock star, an entrepreneur, a manager, an actor and now in his later years an accomplished painter still living in Los Angeles, California.

Tim was born in Prestbury in 1942 and brought up in the family house on Heybridge Lane. Although he attended a prep school in Cumberland and afterwards he went to be privately educated at Strathallan in Scotland, he remembers many happy occasions in the local area. He admits to riding his BSA bicycle to swinging parties in the large houses of the wealthy Prestbury residents, Friday night drinks at the Admiral Rodney and dinner at the Legh Arms with the family that was something of a family tradition. However his abiding passion was for cricket – not only did he love the game but he was also a highly promising player. He captained the Strathallan first eleven in 1958. He remembers playing locally when he had college breaks and scored 47 not out for Prestbury when he was just 13. After a very successful season with Prestbury in 1960 he was invited by Lancashire to join the County Ground Staff and recalls scoring 50 against King's School, Macclesfield. According to Tim he might have been able to make the grade at cricket but his love for music and a visit to Birmingham where he recognised the potential of a pop group, The Moody Blues, and signed them to a contract, put paid to that. They hit the jackpot when their record, *Go Now*, became a huge hit. For Tim it was goodbye to the dream of playing cricket for England and hello USA where he made his home in California.

In the meantime back home in Prestbury the family house at Heybridge Lane was sold to the Plowrights, the Head of Granada Studios.

Tim Hudson's life was now based in the USA and he certainly made the most of it. The 1960s was a magical time for pop music and Tim's easy, wacky style over the air had great appeal for the American audience. British groups were hugely popular and Hudson was prominent in promoting both the Beatles and the Rolling Stones through his radio programme and indeed interviewed the Beatles, projecting them across America. He also managed a band, The Seeds, who epitomised the psychedelic genre of the time and it was about now that Hudson was credited with the phrase for the music of that time, peace, flowers and love – he called it 'Flower Power'. In the mid 1960s he was the undisputed No 1 disc jockey in Hollywood, California and later in the 60s was proud to have promoted Joe

South's song, *Games People Play*, to three Grammy's, including Record of The Year.

Always with an eye for innovation, in the 1970s he started an up market vegetarian restaurant called *The Horticultural Holiday* on Sunset Boulevard. He also gave a course on communications at the Marymount University and later that year his radio station was voted best College Radio Station in the USA. He continued to think outside the box, to use a modern expression and came up with *Hudson's Theatre of the Mind* and later during the 1980s he was nominated for the Peabody award for the special broadcast tribute he gave following the murder of John Lennon in New York.

It was therefore a great surprise when later in the 1980s he left America to return to the UK with wife Maxi and settle down in the Macclesfield countryside, when he bought Birtles Hall, the title 'Lord' and its grounds. It was the start of yet another chapter in the colourful life of this sometimes eccentric but always interesting man.

He set out to create his own idea of paradise; he fashioned out of the ten-acre estate his own cricket ground and built a cricket pavilion

'Lord' Tim Hudson - stetson, blazer, birtles bowel, cricket ground

that was decorated in psychedelic colours and images recreating the music and the flower power era. The Birtles Bowl Cricket ground became famous or infamous in the area depending on your point of view. When Hudson became manager of England's most famous cricketer Ian Botham he set out to fashion him into a marketable image and launch him onto the Hollywood scene. Cream or white stylish Panama hats set off with old fashioned striped cricket jackets or blazers, it was a very fashionable look and Hudson and his entourage tried to get the 'look' established. Regrettably although Botham was a big star in England, cricket and therefore his image had little or no appeal in America and after a series of disagreements and a well-publicised row over an alleged remark from Hudson confiding in the press that Botham took dope, Botham sacked Hudson as his manager and they went their separate ways.

For a time in the eighties Hudson certainly brightened up the British press and the local environs of Macclesfield with tales of what went on at the Birtles Bowl. Cricket was definitely played there but in a style representative of Tim Hudson; Botham definitely appeared and other world cricket stars and a series of celebrities are believed to have played in a variety of matches at the small ground, Viv Richards, Geoff Boycott and Mick Jagger to name just a few. The events always featured music played during the games in a carnival atmosphere of noise and celebration and there were always bevies of young ladies in attendance and Echo and the Bunnymen and Joy Division were alleged to be regular performers. According to Tim half the Australian touring team of 1985 attended one of his parties at Birtles Hall. The local Cheshire country lanes were filled with traffic on the way to and from the ground and the noise and general mayhem broached no favours with Hudson's immediate neighbours. His attempt to bring rock and roll to cricket eventually failed as he fell out with the Macclesfield Council and his neighbours.

He made a number of media appearances and wrote his autobiography, From The Beatles to Botham and all the B-----s In Between; disillusioned with England he returned to California after selling Birtles Hall but retaining the cricket ground.

Throughout the 90s he continued to work in radio but became more and more involved with painting in his own inimitable style.

In the late 1990s the Hudson's, Tim, wife Maxi and one daughter (he has five children) returned to England and Macclesfield in an attempt to restore the paradise, the glory and to bring back the 'Camelot' days of the Birtles Bowl. After a long and fruitless struggle with opposition from neighbours and the Macclesfield Planners the Hudsons gave up the struggle, put the cricket ground on the market (it was sold in 2007) and in 2004 once again returned to Palm Springs, USA.

Tim continued with his art and his paintings are now exhibited in several venues in America and he has embarked on a number of painting tours throughout the USA, indeed his most recent tour was in 2008. Tim never short to self publicise says that Mel Gibson, Joan Collins and Shaft and several other Hollywood celebrities own his paintings and he has appeared in *Vogue* magazine and was likened to the painter Jackson Pollack by the *Los Angeles* magazine.

At the age of 66 one would think that he would be slowing down – but not Tim Hudson. In May 2008 he surfaced once again in the *Macclesfield Express* during a flying visit to the town with his wife and told readers that he was here to appear on Bollington's Canalside Community Radio station and simultaneously broadcast to his radio station in Los Angeles. "We'll take the best of the British music scene to LA and bring Macclesfield the American hits" he explained. (It was planned to produce the linkup in October 2008). He went on to explain that he had always wanted his own radio station here in Macclesfield but was informed that it just wasn't possible.

'Lord' Tim Hudson is most definitely a character with very many strings to his bow: self-styled 'Lord', millionaire, painter, rock manager, top DJ, original hippy and actor, he was the voice of Tom in Walt Disney's *The Aristocats* and the eagle in *Jungle Book*. Despite his great success in America he still regularly returns to Macclesfield. There must be something about the town to be able to compete with California and the magic of Los Angeles, Palm Springs and San Francisco – after all Tim Hudson has the choice and keeps returning!

Geoff Lloyd – DJ, Radio Presenter

Geoff currently hosting, *The Geoff Show*, on Absolute Radio (formerly Virgin Radio) is much more than a disc jockey and is perhaps better described as an award winning radio presenter playing music whilst at the same time offering chat and interest on a variety of listener conscious subjects; nevertheless his basis is music.

Although Geoff was born in Withington near Manchester the family moved to Macclesfield just two months after his birth. He grew up in Hatton Street, which was next to the old Labour Exchange, and

Geoff Lloyd

attended Byron Street Primary that was later merged with others to form St Barnabus. His father was a postman at Macclesfield sorting station and his mother was a nurse at the old Infirmary and then at West Park and Moss Lane Hospital.

At the age of 11 the family moved to Lyme Avenue, just off London Road. Geoff did well at school and was offered a place at King's School but after a short spell there, he says that he never really settled down, he transferred to Ryles Park School. After leaving school at the age of 16 he had several attempts at employment as he searched to establish a career path. At various times he worked at Burton's Menswear in Mill Street, Lukic Belgrade Hotel, Bollington, the printers Williamson and Cooper on London Road and eventually found a niche that suited his needs; he got a job at Margin Music in King Edward Street.

Whilst at school he had tried to get into the music business via local radio. At the tender age of 14 he volunteered to work at Macclesfield's hospital radio station called Bedside Radio and that gave him the taste to later volunteer to work at the only radio station in the area, Piccadilly Radio, Manchester. However, Geoff had greater determination than to just accept small crumbs off the table and, at the age of 16, started his own mobile disco and was delighted to be appointed the resident DJ at Macclesfield Rugby Club. It was a start and gave him the opportunity to establish a patter and perform in front of a live audience – all good experience.

He started to move up the ladder when, at the age of eighteen, he started work at KFM Radio in Stockport, which in time would become Signal Radio Cheshire, and was given his own show to host. For a time life was hectic but Geoff felt able to leave the family home in Macclesfield and rent a bed-sit in nearby Heaton Moor, financed by his combined earnings from the radio show, the mobile disco and a part-time job reading travel reports on the AA's Roadwatch service programme in Cheadle Hulme.

In 1995 circumstances forced him into moving back to Macclesfield to live with his parents and back to his old job at Margin Music. Nevertheless, he still nurtured a desire for a career in radio and became involved with the campaign to establish Macclesfield's first and only radio station Silk FM. His persistence paid off and in 1996 he started work for Piccadilly Key 103 radio, covering the Manchester area, and once again had to leave the family environ in Macclesfield and move to the Manchester area, this time for good.

His show with a co-presenter, *The Pete & Geoff Show*, ran for more than ten years and during that period was taken over by Virgin Radio and was changed from an afternoon show to a breakfast show. The music and the chat perpetrated by the duo ranged across a whole series of topics and its irreverence earned a huge following, so much so that in 1998 it achieved The Silver Sony Radio Award and, in 2002, attained the ultimate radio accolade, The Gold Sony Award for the Best Daily Music Programme.

However, in 2006, the format was changed and Geoff took over as the sole presenter in *The Geoff Show*. He proved that he had not lost his touch when, in 2007, he was named Best Radio Personality at the European Radio Awards at a lavish ceremony in Barcelona; he was at the top of his profession.

Geoff Lloyd has several strings to his bow and, as well as a number of voice over presentations including The Post Office, he has written his own radio scripts and has many television appearances on his CV.

His script writing credits include *TFI Friday*, *The Mrs Merton Show* and *Comic Relief* for the BBC.

His expertise in his trade is much sought after, as indicated by the demand for his services, as a contributor on such programmes as *The Story of Light Entertainment*, *My God I'm My Dad*, *Celebrity Scandal*, *100 Greatest Albums*, *It Shouldn't Happen – Awards*, *The Culture of the 70s, 80s, 90s*, *The Golden Rules of Comedy*, and *Madonna vs. Queen Mania*. His popularity, knowledge and easy manner have also made him a popular studio guest on programmes such as *Big Brothers Little Brother* and *Big Brothers Efourum* as a regular guest and he has made appearances on *Sitcom Showdown* and *Richard and Judy*.

Macclesfield can be proud of one of its sons whose hard work and determination has propelled him to the top of his profession and he still returns to the town, where he was brought up and educated, to visit family and attend family functions.

Peter Forbes Robinson – Opera Singer

Unquestionably, Peter Frobes Robinson is the finest opera singer Macclesfield has ever produced, a singer who went on to perform all over the world and has been recognised as one of the greatest British bass singers..

He was born Peter Robinson in Macclesfield on 21st May, 1926 and the family, father Wilfred and mother Gertrude, lived in High Street and then moved to Park Lane when Wilfred became a manager at Burden's grocery store.

Peter was educated first of all at St George's Primary School where he sang in the choir at the Sunday church services and was later a member of the Youth Fellowship Group. Joan Swindells, a long time Macclesfield resident, remembers Peter well from those Fellowship days and recalls one night in a meeting during the war when black out was in force and the youngsters told each other ghost stories. Peter told his own story so well that he frightened himself so much that someone had to walk him home!

Exposed to the church environment, it became clear from an early age that Peter had singing in his blood. He sang in the St George's Musical Society Male Voice Choir that was based at Lord Street Large Sunday School and enjoyed performing with the Gilbert and Sullivan Society. His brother Roy was an organist at Christ Church in Macclesfield.

After leaving St George's Primary School, Peter attended King's School where his height and weight enabled him to excel at rugby and he was later invited to perform in trials for the Cheshire Youth team. He also joined the King's School's Combined Cadet Force (CCF), where he excelled in the parades when throwing the baton!

After completing his education at King's School he attended St Paul's College, Cheltenham ostensibly to undertake teacher training. During this time in his life he still retained an interest in the army and in 1946, as a volunteer, he became a Captain in the Royal Army Engineering Corp, a post he held until 1948. He graduated to Loughborough College where in 1949-50 he obtained an Hons Diploma in physical education.

For a time he taught physical education at the Central School in Macclesfield where some pupils regarded him as severe in his application of disciplines, whereas others found him to be kind and considerate. Local man, Ken Whittaker, remembers him as a jovial character and shared with him many an enjoyable pint in the Bate Hotel.

It was a busy but eventful time in his life and in 1952 he married Marion Stubbs but any pretence at settling down into a cosy domestic life was about to be blown sky high; their lives would change and change for ever.

During his time teaching at the Central School Peter continued singing locally at his church and in local concert performances and

Peter Forbes Robinson

then one day decided to enter a talent competition that was looking for the next Mario Lanza. Lanza at the time was a hugely successful singer who had been able to marry classical singing with that of popular music and he had developed into a major Hollywood singing/acting movie star. The competition was held in London and broadcast over the radio. Joan and husband Ron Swindells, friends of Peter, remember listening to the competition and were thrilled when the winner was announced, "Peter Robinson from Macclesfield".

The event, the result, would change his life and send him into a totally new career direction. The prize was to study in Italy at La Scuola di Canto in Milan, where he would train, study and practice for twelve months. After completing the course he returned to England and became a professional opera singer adding Forbes to his name, perhaps to make it more professional.

In 1954 he had the honour of becoming the Principal Artist – bass, at the Royal Opera House, Covent Garden a position he would retain until 1983!

During his long and distinguished career he made four solo albums, several television appearances including the production of several videos and a recording with Sir Colin Davis of Britten's *Peter Grimes* as well as appearing in concerts all over the world.

At various times he was the guest artist in Dublin, at Sadler's Wells, Opera North, Scottish and Welsh National Opera Companies as well as performing in Barcelona, Edinburgh, Holland, Leeds, Lucerne, Ottawa, Portugal, Argentina, Belgium, Canada, Denmark, France, Germany, Italy, Luxembourg, Sweden, America, South Korea, Japan and South Africa; he was much in demand performing works by Mozart, Verdi, Benjamin Britten and other renowned composers.

Although his career and performances had very many highlights two received special recognition, he received the Opera Medal in 1963 for creating the title role in Michael Tippett's *King Priam* and became the first British singer in 100 years to sing *Don Giovanni* at the Royal Opera House, Covent Garden. It was fitting when, in 1979, his old university, Loughborough, awarded him an Honourable Doctor of Literature (Hon Litt D).

He did return to Macclesfield from time to time and once performed at the Majestic cinema theatre and Macclesfield residents, Derek and Margaret Way, recalled an occasion when they had a drink with him at the Midland Hotel, Manchester while he was appearing in *Madame Butterfly* at the Palace Theatre.

For much of his professional life he lived in London and during his leisure time he told the press that his hobbies were walking, talking, gardening, jazz and croquet.

Tragically, at the comparatively early age of 61, he died of a heart attack on 13th May, 1987, in his parked car whilst his wife shopped.

He was for his time a truly great opera singer who could count appearances at Covent Garden and Sadler's Wells with the supreme accolade of starring at La Scala, Milan as testimony to his standing in his profession.

To think that this all stemmed from his early days at St George's choir!

Entertainers and Media Figures

Today there is a fine line between entertainers – actors and movie stars – and media figures such as radio programme or television presenters, who regularly appear on our screens or in our homes and become almost like fixtures in our daily lives. It becomes harder to separate the actors from the presenters; after all both are providing entertainment and are seeking our approval.

For most of us it becomes a little more entertaining and interesting when you are aware or realise that the man or woman appearing on your television screen, or the person whose voice is coming directly to you through the radio, was actually born in your hometown.

Helen Atkinson Wood – Actress and Presenter

A talented highly versatile actress who has performed in comedy, serious drama and has also developed into a much in demand television presenter and writer was once Head Girl at Macclesfield High School.

Helen Atkinson-Wood was born in Cheadle Hulme on 14th March, 1955 and came to Macclesfield in 1956 where her father Frederick ran his business, British Crepe, in Jordangate. The family lived in Tytherington and Helen went to school firstly at Beech Lane Primary and then on to Macclesfield High School. It was during her time at the High School, and after a visit to the King's School where she appeared in a production of *Twelfth Night*, that she first got her impetus to go on the stage. It was also during her time at the school and following a very serious accident, when she was thrown from a horse and spent many months learning to walk again, that she earned the respect and the friendship of King's School pupil Ian Curtis, who would go on to music stardom with Joy Division before tragically committing suicide at the age of 23. Helen was a bright student and left Macclesfield for London University to study drama only to realise that teaching was not for her and transferred to Oxford University where she studied fine art. However, when she joined the drama society at the university she found herself working with fellow students Rowan Atkinson and Richard Curtis, who would later feature large in her life.

She appeared at the Edinburgh Fringe Festival with Rowan Atkinson

Helen Atkinson Wood

and was later joined by a young man called Ben Elton who would feature greatly in both of their lives.

Four young men from Oxford started a parody about a radio station and asked Helen to join them. They called it *Radio Active*, and toured Australia and New Zealand with the show collecting numerous awards on the way, before its success was recognised and the programme, transferred and adapted to television, was broadcast as *KYTV*. So popular was it that it collected a Montreux Silver Rose for Light Entertainment and a Best Comedy Award.

Helen was now on the way to recognition, especially following her success as a regular presenter on the ground breaking, sometimes controversial television show *OTT (Over The Top)* – which it often was; she shared the spotlight with Chris Tarrant and Lenny Henry. Helen's comedic abilities and her gift of timing earned her a role in the wacky, controversial television show *The Young Ones* and she followed that with a West End debut in the play *Silly Cow*; both shows were written

by Ben Elton who clearly had a great regard for Helen's talents. However, perhaps her signature role came in 1987 with the hugely successful television series *Blackadder*, written by old friends Richard Curtis, Rowan Atkinson and Ben Elton. Rowan Atkinson was the star but in series three, *Blackadder The Third*, in 1987, Elton created a role for Helen with the comic character Mrs Miggins.

Helen's versatility can be illustrated by the fact that she has twice been nominated by The British Comedy Awards as Top Female Performer but has also appeared in many West End and other theatre productions: Alan Ayckbourn's *Time and Time Again*, *Blithe Spirit*, she played Viola in *Twelfth Night*, Polina in Chekov's The *Seagull*,

Clive Anderson and Helen, Co presenters, Private Lives

The Magistrate, The Moonstone and *High Places* and has starred in the television drama *Your Cheatin' Heart*, to name just a few.

On one occasion in 2003, when she was starring in a three month engagement at the Royal Exchange Theatre in Manchester, Helen returned to the King's School Girl's Division (High School now defunct) where her desire was first inspired, to give a master-class on a career in acting.

Over the past few years Helen has shrewdly diversified her talents to embrace television presenting across the various TV companies: *Collector's Lot, Style Trial, Gourmet Guide, Al Fresco, Good Food Live,* have revealed and highlighted her versatility and more recently she has co-presented *Private Lives* with Clive Anderson.

Her sharp mind and ready wit means that she is a regular and popular guest on a whole series of programmes ranging from *Call My Bluff, Have I Got News For You, Food and Drink* and *This Morning* and she recently guest starred with an audio appearance in *Doctor Who*. She gives talks on food and wine, the *Blackadder* series and lectures on careers in the theatre and is in demand for voice-overs and still finds time to write on travel for the *Daily Mail!*

In 2008 she appeared in documentaries celebrating the 25th anniversary of the launching of the *Blackadder* series in 1983.

Although Helen lives in London with husband writer John Morton she says that she will always have a soft spot for Macclesfield in her heart. She does return from time to time and regards herself very much as a Cheshire girl. She told me very proudly that she was once Miss East Cheshire Pony Club! Never mind a Montreux Silver Rose!

Johnny Maxfield – Actor

Johnny Heywood was born in a terraced cottage in Bank Street Macclesfield in 1931 to parents Alfred, a train driver and Hilda a former Stockport mill worker. Tragically for his parents, Johnny was the only child from nine births who lived beyond the age of twelve months! His mother was stoic and made of stern stuff and for a number of years she was a housekeeper for a wealthy Macclesfield family before her sense of justice manifested itself in an interest in politics. For more than 17 years she gave service to the town as a Labour Councillor.

Young John was educated at St Paul's Primary School before moving on to secondary education at the Central School. Like most at the time, his formal education ended at the tender age of 14 and he went to work as an apprentice mechanic but decided that his love of soccer on a Saturday afternoon took preference over his employers work requirements, so he left. Perhaps influenced by his father, at the age of 15 he joined the railways.

On 29th March, 1952 he married Brenda and in 1954 they had their first son Trevor followed by David in 1955. After just a few short years on the railways he was made redundant, in 1963, in the Beecham reorganisation when many thousands lost their jobs. It was a tough time for John and his growing family and he was prepared to turn his hand to any job in order to put food on the table.

However, the turning point in his life came when he joined the Royal Engineers and was able to pursue his long felt dream to go on the stage and entertain. His chance came when troops were being demobbed and he was able to perform on stage at the several formal concerts organised for the departing men. It was good early experience and he quickly discovered that he had a gift for regional dialects.

In 1975 he started the daunting job as a semi-professional stand-up comic with overtones of George Formby in his act; he had adopted the stage name of Maxfield after his mother's maiden name and so the dye was cast.

Never shy at coming forward Johnny's persistence paid off and in the mid 70s he received his first television speaking part on *Coronation Street* playing a court reporter. He quickly established a friendship with Bill Toomey (Jack Duckworth in the soap) that was to last a lifetime. Over the years *Coronation Street* was kind to Johnny and he made nine appearances in a variety of roles.

Other television credits involved appearances in *The Onedin Line, Emmerdale Farm, Brookside, Cardiac* and *Hetty Wainthropp Investigates*. However, he still performed his own act and often featured an old Shirley Bassey favourite, *The Party's Over*. He also featured in the Richard Gere film *Yanks*, but sadly his part was edited out so he was not seen in the eventual launch of the blockbuster.

However, the role that made him an iconic feature of the 1970s and late into the 80s came in what at first appeared to be a modest television advertisement for Heinz Soup.

The job was advertised and an estimated 1500 applicants auditioned for the part of an ideal granddad promoting Heinz soup along with an ideal grandson. At the time, with his silvery hair and confident exterior, Johnny did not represent the stereotypical granddad with slippers and cardigan, therefore to enable himself to look a little older he removed his dentures before going in front of the cameras and got the part.

Johnny and his young 'grandson' Adam Sunderland featured in the highly popular advertisement throughout the rest of the 70s and most of the 80s. The dialogue and interplay between the pair endeared them to the viewing millions. It made Johnny a most recognisable face on our screens for all those years. At one time Heinz let him go and Batchelor's soups snapped him up before Heinz realised the error of their ways and re-employed him. In May 1992, Heinz started a new campaign with Johnny, now almost 62, leading the shoot at Pinewood Studios.

Although he was the perfect television granddad he was much better in real life as a granddad to one grandson and two granddaughters.

Sadly over the years Johnny had experienced heart problems but had been able to cope and his family were always there for him. Once again in the 2000s *Coronation Street* approached him to make yet another appearance but he declined believing that his failing eyesight might let him down.

In April 2002 Johnny Maxfield had a heart attack that sadly proved to be the last he would suffer and he later died from the complications. His grieving family managed to trace Adam Sunderland, who had also achieved fame from their national Heinz advertisement, and he was able to pay his last respects to his television 'granddad' at the moving funeral ceremony.

He was clearly a very popular man with time and a joke for every one and every occasion and was often involved in charitable works for which he sought no recompense; a real son of Macclesfield who created a 'national niche' for himself.

Marshall Lancaster – Actor
Born in Macclesfield on 5th October, 1974 and educated at Tytherington High School, Marshall Lancaster is an actor who already has amassed an impressive array of roles in television, stage and film and appears to be well on the way to wider acclaim in the years ahead.

He got his basic grounding in local theatre with the SCAMPS Youth Company and the Macclesfield Amateur Dramatic Society, where he featured in *Don't Forget Your Trousers* in 1992 playing a gorillagram, *Blood Brothers* in 1993 and the Paragon Youth Theatre, where in 1995 he played Herr Schultz in *Cabaret.*

As most aspiring actors have to, Marshall took on an array of day jobs between seeking acting roles.

His first break into television came in 1997 when he appeared in *Family Affairs*, a programme that ran until 2005 and at last gave him something recognisable to put on his CV. Soon he was appearing in cameo roles in some of our best loved and most popular television series, *Where The Heart Lies, Casualty, The Bill, Holby City, Peak Practice* and *Doctors* as well as appearances in, *The Lakes, Grease Monkeys* and several others. He also managed

Marshall Lancaster as 'Slug'

to get parts in the films *The Wedding Tackle, Aberdeen in 2000* and *Blow Dry* in 2001.

It was while working at a warehouse loading up milk vans for morning deliveries that Marshall was called for the interview that was to launch his career into orbit. He auditioned for and obtained the part of Detective Constable, Chris Skelton in the BBC television series *Life On Mars*. The first series in 2006 proved to be extremely popular winning both Bafta and Emmy awards and this science fiction, time travel crime series was also sold to America and Australia. The first series ran for sixteen episodes and, although it had great audience figures, Marshall could not take anything for granted in this most precarious of professions. He started to take a plastering course in order to shore up his earnings. In the meantime in 2007 he obtained a part in the ever-popular soap *Coronation Street* appearing as the character layabout 'Slug.' His character enjoyed a very strong story line keeping Lancaster well to the fore in the soap throughout 2009. His double dealing against old friend Becky, wife of landlord Steve, ran for several weeks enhancing his reputation as a 'villain'.

Showing that there is more than one string to his bow, Marshall also appeared on stage in 2007 in the May production of *Up 'n' Under* at the Thameside Hippodrome and also performed in *Wuthering Heights* at the York Theatre Royal.

During the early stages of his *Coronation Street* run, Marshall was also in the middle of his plasterer's course when he had a call to tell him that there was to be a second series of *Life On Mars* and the show came to our screens again in 2007.

There was even more joy for his career when the success of *Life On Mars* resulted in a spin off series, *Ashes to Ashes*, featuring virtually the same cast, that came to our screens to great acclaim in 2008.

In the summer of 2008 he appeared again in York, this time at the National Railway Museum in a production of *The Railway Children*.

Despite his success and the steady climb towards public recognition in a high profile career Marshall Lancaster appears to be well adjusted with his feet firmly placed on the ground.

He lives quietly with his partner, has a bull-dog terrier, likes tropical fish, driving, and all sports and is an avid fan of Macclesfield FC. He has run in the Great North Run to support the Marie Curie Cancer Care Trust and a unique feature of his personal appearance is that one eye is green and the other is blue!

It appears that Marshall Lancaster is set to become a national star and indeed in 2009 he once again adorned our television screens starring in an ITV sitcom playing the part of 'Pete' in *Boy Meets Woman*.

Nick Robinson – Presenter BBC Political Editor

He is on our television screens almost every night in his distinctive, rather severe, dark glasses and even more distinct balding head – a very familiar figure. Succinct, knowledgeable and highly professional he is much respected and at the top of his profession as the political head of BBC television.

Nicholas Anthony Robinson was born in Macclesfield on 5th October, 1963 to parents Eustace Desmond Robinson, a civil engineer and Evelyn Ruth Robinson and they lived at 54, Legh Road, Prestbury.

Before graduating to Oxford, where he studied philosophy, politics and economics, he attended Cheadle Hulme School where at the age of eight he met Will Redhead, son of the legendary broadcaster Brian Redhead. Nick became a frequent visitor to the Redhead family home in Rainow as his friendship blossomed with Will.

His career might never have taken place if he had not survived a terrible car crash in France in 1982 in which his very close friends

James Nelson and Will Redhead were killed. It was Brian Redhead who would later encourage and almost mentor Nick to enter journalism as a career. The crash left Nick with severe burns but a year later he was fit enough to go to Oxford and commence his studies.

1986 was perhaps the pivotal moment in his career. He spent that year as national chairman of the Young Conservatives and was so involved and passionate that he was called the 'Blue Robbo' but he also joined the BBC as a production trainee after working for Piccadilly Radio in Manchester.

Behind the scenes he helped produce such television and radio programmes as *Brass Tacks, This Week, Next Week, Newsround* and *Crimewatch UK*, all the time acquiring experience. He moved on to join *On The Record*, as an assistant producer before becoming deputy editor and later moving to the much-respected *Panorama* programme as deputy editor, a post that he held for three years.

Confident in his ability, he first went in front of the cameras in

Nick Robinson – BBC's Political Editor

1996 as a political correspondent and in 1997 covered his first General Election for BBC Radio. However, he went behind the scenes again when presenting for BBC Radio 5 live *Weekend Breakfast* and *Late Night Live* – he was at this stage nothing if not versatile!

From 1999 through to October 2002 he was the BBC News's chief political correspondent and also presented *Westminster Live* on BBC Two before leaving the BBC to join Independent Television as the ITV News's Political Editor.

He has a very distinctive style direct: concise and seemingly without prejudice. This direct honesty does not always sit well, especially with the politicians. When in August 2005 Andrew Marr left the BBC they moved quickly to re-employ Nick Robinson as Political Editor – ITV were devastated.

2005 also saw Nick made his mark when challenging a deliberate attempt by labour to smear the conservatives with a Labour Party poster alleging that the Conservative Party would cut services by £3.5 billion if elected. Robinson tore holes in the statement when confronting Prime Minister Tony Blair, who was forced to concede that the figure was misleading, apparently to the amusement of Gordon Brown. In another memorable interview with deputy Prime Minister John Prescott regarding the honesty of Labour's 2005 manifesto, Prescott was seen on camera mouthing "fucking pillock" as Robinson persisted with his questions.

No respecter of persons, Nick also had a well-publicised run in with President George Bush, who on several occasions did not relish his direct questioning. On one occasion, after being pricked by a question, he said to Robinson "You should cover up your bald head, it's getting hot" Nick quickly responded "I didn't know you cared". Bush retorted "I don't". No covering over the cracks there then.

Two years later they had another confrontation at Camp David in America. President Bush on sighting Robinson's distinctive features sneered at him "You still hanging around".

Today Nick Robinson is the established face of the BBC political news and his very frequent reports are succinct, very clear and entertaining. He asks the questions that the viewers would ask. He has also lightened his approach and has appeared on such popular programmes as *Have I Got News For You* and *Children in Need.* He lives with his wife and three children in London, where he enjoys theatre going, but his heart is still in the north with his beloved Manchester United.

Brian Redhead – Broadcaster

For many people the late Brian Redhead, throughout the 1970s and well into the 80s, was the doyen of broadcasters easily identified by his gingery, sometimes shaggy beard and distinctive voice; an accomplished writer, journalist, author and above all a very capable broadcaster with a large and loyal band of listeners. He was also a mentor of the BBC's Nick Robinson, encouraging the young aspiring journalist, although their political views were very opposite.

Redhead was not a Maxonian but we have every right to regard him as an adopted son. During his broadcasts he frequently referred to the North West in glowing terms and in particular Manchester and Macclesfield came in for regular praise.

He was born, Brian Leonard Redhead in Newcastle-upon-Tyne on 28th December, 1929 and died in Macclesfield on 23rd January, 1994 at the comparatively early age of 64. His father, Ernest Leonard Redhead, was a silkscreen printer before becoming an advertising agent and his mother was Janet Crossley (nee Fairley). Redhead was a keen and bright student and after leaving the Royal Grammar School in Newcastle he graduated, after National Service, to read history at Cambridge University.

1954 was a momentous year in his life because not only did he marry wife Jean Salmon (Jenni) on June 19 but he also commenced what would be a long and successful career as a journalist for the *Manchester Guardian*, now known simply as *The Guardian*. However, in the early 1960s he left *The Guardian* and moved with his family to London where he joined the BBC's *Tonight* television programme.

Their stay was brief and within twelve months he was back in his beloved north rejoining *The Guardian*.

He served his time gaining valuable experience and in 1965 was appointed Northern Editor of *The Guardian* and in 1969 took on the role of editor of the *Manchester Evening News*. During this time his family had grown to include three sons Stephen, James and William who was a twin of sister Annabel. They lived in Cheadle Hulme where the Redheads, despite Brian's perceived political opinion, sent their children to a fee-paying school.

However a pivotal and decisive moment in his career came in 1975 when he was unsuccessful in his application to fill the vacancy of editor of *The Guardian*. He decided on a change of direction and joined BBC Radio 4 to replace the highly popular Robert Robinson on the *Today* programme.

Once again it meant upheaval in his personal life. By now he was living in Calrofold Lane, Rainow, Macclesfield and the transfer to the BBC meant a return to London, not his favourite place. He solved the problem by commuting to London and maintaining a flat in the Barbican, an arrangement that would last for more than eighteen years.

His routine meant departing from Macclesfield Railway Station every Monday night always observing, as he stepped into the train, the distinctive clock tower on the Church of St Michaels's and All Angels that dominated the sky-line, to commence his weekly sojourn to London. He couldn't wait for the weekends to return to Macclesfield and his Rainow cottage with its thick, solid, stone walls and small windows. He particularly loved the addition of a conservatory that gave him the feeling of being permanently in the countryside, which he wrote of, loved and championed so much, surrounded as it was by flowers in the summertime and very often the cosiness of snow in the winter.

He believed that the time and opportunity was worth the inconvenience as he had experience in front of the television cameras having presented *Points North* and on the radio had also chaired *A Word In Edgeways*, so he was familiar and at ease with the art of communication and ready for the new challenge.

His style was complemented perfectly with John Timpson, his fellow presenter, in a partnership that would last for more than ten years. Their humour was laconic, topical and warm despite the fact that in many ways socially and politically they were very different. Although they disagreed on many issues they had a great affection and respect for each other.

Brian was what one could call left wing, not terribly enamoured with the conservative party and often gave guest Tory politicians a hard time. He gave the Conservative Chancellor of the time, Nigel Lawson, a direct dressing down on air for daring to suggest that he knew how Redhead voted and on another occasion he had a similar set to with the then Trade and Industry Secretary, Peter Lilley.

He was, however, well respected by the Tory party and Prime Minister Margaret Thatcher paid him the unique compliment of telephoning his programme directly from her office in Downing Street.

Colleagues regarded Redhead as a typical, blunt, cocky, forthright self-made northerner always seeking to fight a cause and to eradicate injustice and regarded Timpson as a middle class conservative

St Michael's and All Angels Church

southerner with old style values. Nevertheless, despite their differences, the warmness of their relationship was typified by their shared sense of humour. Traffic problems were often featured and jokes made of the usual and regular problems even establishing a mythical 'The Friends of the M6'. United in their suffering they also talked of 'The League of Pear Shaped Men' with themselves as the principal members. Redhead was never afraid to be controversial and defend his beloved north. On one memorable occasion he told listeners when giving a forecast that the weather would be 'brighter in the north than the south, like the people'.

Despite his alleged political leanings he did confess that he had cast a vote for the Conservative MP for Macclesfield, Nicholas Winterton (now Sir). It was typical of Redhead to vote for the man rather than the doctrine.

At the height of his popularity tragedy struck the family when, in 1982 in a car crash in France, their youngest son William aged 18 died. It was a devastating blow and Brian sought comfort in religion and became a confirmed member of the Church of England. He started to charter the history of the bible in his Radio 4 series *The Good Book* and it was believed that he might in retirement perhaps train as an Anglican priest. During this time of tragedy the village of Rainow rallied round the Redheads who were regular members of the congregation at the Holy Trinity Church in the village; Brian often would read the lesson and the family would attend the Christmas Eve midnight service.

When the First Gulf War broke out in 1991 he volunteered as a presenter on the BBC Radio 4 News FM service. However his health started to deteriorate in 1993 and, despite early hopes that he would overcome the toxin that was poisoning his system, he took leave from the *Today* programme in December in the full expectation that his health problems would be sorted out and he would return to work in the new year. Sadly it was not to be and the world was shocked to learn of his premature death on 23rd January, 1994. Macclesfield regarded him with such affection that the flag on the Town Hall mast was flown at half-mast as the news became known.

At his funeral at the Holy Trinity Church, Rainow daughter Abby gave the reading and amongst the many mourners were old BBC colleagues John Cole and John Humphreys; Redhead's ashes were scattered around the grounds of his beloved Rainow cottage.

He was a great northerner and a great champion of Macclesfield. On several occasions during his national programmes he would mention the town, the Silk Museum, Gawsworth Hall, the Peak District, Macclesfield Forest and on one famous occasion he told of seeing an old space shuttle covered in stickers from people around the world and one said, he told his listeners, "Follow me and Macclesfield Town".

He was more than just a broadcaster and became somewhat of an institution, leaving behind a legacy of values; he was a great champion of the Heritage Centre, the Museum and East Cheshire Hospice and has left his broadcasts and a number of books to vouch for his ideals.

His abiding love was for the countryside. Today with the great concern over global warming, the survival of animals, habitat and ultimately mankind, Brian Redhead had this to say, in 1992, in his book *Months In The Country* about the need to preserve the countryside and stressing how vital farming was, "If wildlife is to survive in Britain we need to graze meadows and moorland, manage woodlands and hedgerows and excavate ponds. The creatures cannot do it for themselves. Only we can".

There is also a fitting memorial to him, one whose usefulness would undoubtedly appeal and warm him. It is the Brian Redhead Court, a building offering two blocks containing 64 flats on the City Campus in Hulme, Manchester for the housing of postgraduate students, their partners and families.

Jenni Murray, OBE – Broadcaster

Born in Barnsley on 12th May, 1950 to parents Alvin and Win, Jennifer Bailey endured a difficult relationship with her mother, who made no secret of the fact that she would have preferred a son, that perhaps influenced her opinions for the rest of her life. She adored her father and later in life wrote a book *Memoirs of a Not So Dutiful Daughter*, detailing and attempting to understand the lack of warmth in the relationship with her mother.

Jennifer was educated at Barnsley High before graduating to Hull University, where she studied French and Drama with early aspirations to become an actress or journalist. She never felt appreciated by her mother and was unsurprisingly hurt when her father was sent abroad to work for several years and her mother elected to go with him leaving Jennifer in the care of her grandmother. Perhaps it was of no surprise then, that Jennifer grew up a rebel. As a 21 years old student she married Brian Murray but sadly the marriage was short lived and in 1973 she joined the BBC in Bristol as a local junior reporter. She gained experience working in Leeds with *Look North* then moved to Southampton as a reporter in the early 1980s, where she met and fell in love with David Forgham. Her career was on the rise and she joined the *Newsnight* team and also became a presenter on Radio 4's *Today*, working with fellow Rainow resident Brian Redhead. However her zenith was reached when, in 1987, she commenced as presenter on the hugely popular, *Woman's Hour*, a position that she holds still today.

She shortened her name to Jenni but retained her married name of Murray and despite her fame and popularity her mother's animosity to her never changed.

Jenni however maintained her own very strong opinions on marriage and euthanasia for which she has occasionally been pilloried. She wrote an article that was taken to be anti-marriage and the *Daily Mail* described her as "the most dangerous woman in Britain". The *Evening Standard* produced a billboard proclaiming 'Woman's Hour presenter says marriage is legalised prostitution'. Nevertheless Jenni had lived with David Forgham for more than twenty years without a marriage certificate and had produced two sons.

In 2005, strictly, she claims due to legal reasons and in particular the inheritance tax laws, she decided to marry. David and Jenni were married at Macclesfield Register Office attended by her two sons and Norma a friend. However, she had all sentimental and romantic references removed from the service, there was no mention of bride and groom, no flowers or music and no till death us do part. She confirmed that the marriage was purely because of legal reasons and the ceremony had no influence on her love for David.

In terms of her career she was awarded the accolade of UK Broadcaster of the Year for 1998 and in 1999 was appointed OBE for her services to broadcasting.

For many years, similar to Brian Redhead, she has commuted by train from her family home 'Wuthering Heights' in Rainow to stay in her tiny London basement flat that she called 'Wuthering Depths', when broadcasting from the capital.

Marriage and a career at its very peak resulted in a softening of her mother's attitude to her without full acceptance but Jenni's endurance was about to be tested to the full. In 2006 her beloved father died and her mother, after a short illness and a coming together with Jenni, also died on 20th December of that year. On 21st December, 2006 Jenni announced during *Woman's Hour* that she had been diagnosed with breast cancer. She told the listeners "I've known about the diagnosis for a couple of weeks now. It was diagnosed up in Macclesfield when I was supposedly on my holidays. Treatments are very good these days and I know quite a bit about this disease thanks to working on the programme. Fingers crossed everything should be all right".

She had known about her condition while comforting her dying mother – truly a testing time.

Jenni Murray is not one to be pitied and in 2008 she made the headlines when confronting a squatter in her London flat, far from being intimidated she made him clean the place up before calling the police!

During an interview with the *Daily Telegraph* in July 2008 she told the reporter that because of complications following her chemotherapy she had difficulty in walking due to problems with her hips and had to rely on crutches. She was still travelling to London three days a week to broadcast but confessed "Walking to the train to go home to Macclesfield is like climbing Everest for me".

She concluded the interview by stating, "The only thing I can do now is say "Yes, I've got cancer like thousands of other women. All I can do is put my trust in a good oncologist, try to lose weight, and try to forget about it".

Let's hope that the good country fresh air of Rainow continues to contribute to her recovery.

Jenni Murray is also the author of *Is It Me Or Is It Hot In Here, That's My Boy* and *The Woman's Hour: A History of Women in Britain since the Second World War*.

Michael Jackson – Ex Controller, BBC Television

Michael Jackson has the distinction of being the first media studies graduate to attain a senior rank in the British media and indeed is only one of three people to have become controller of BBC One and BBC Two, the senior television channels of the BBC. If that were not enough his career record also reveals that he became Chief Executive of another major British television company, Channel 4, a position he held from 1997-2001.

Born in the sub district of Congleton in the registration district of Macclesfield on 11th February, 1958 to Ernest Jackson a master baker and wife Margaret formerly Kearsley, he was brought up in the family house Greenwayes, Gawsworth Road, Macclesfield. Michael was educated at King's School, Macclesfield and was set on a career in the media from the age of 12! After leaving King's School he went to the Polytechnic in Central London where he graduated with a First Class Honours BA in Media Studies. It was the first degree course of its kind ever to be held in Britain.

During his course he wrote a paper on the need for a fourth television channel in the UK and shortly after leaving University he found himself as the organiser of The Channel Four. It comprised a group of television producers who lobbied the government ceaselessly, arguing that there was a need for a new independent station to challenge the BBC and ITV companies.

Success was achieved in 1982 when the new company was launched and Michael Jackson became producer of one of its first major series, *The Sixties*, a documentary that proved to be very successful.

He moved to Beat Productions and continued to make programmes for Channel 4: *Open The Box*, an in depth study of how television programmes were made and the immensely successful *The Media*

Show where as founding editor he earned a resounding accolade from Waldemar Januszczak, of *The Guardian* newspaper who, in 1997, said that that show was "one of the defining television programmes of the 1980s", he went further and said "In Michael Jackson, its first producer, it gave us a media-genius" – praise indeed. His ability and skills soon came to the notice of the major channels and in 1988 he was lured away to the BBC2 by Controller Alan Yentob, who quickly put him in charge of a new late-night arts programme *The Late Show*, which was launched in January 1989. Many people doubted the venture and sceptics claimed that it was ambitious to run such a programme four nights a week (after *Newsnight*) and that Yentob was placing a lot of finance and self ego as well as faith in his young producer. There was a great deal of pressure on the young Michael Jackson.

The programme proved to be a huge success and ran for six years and, in 2003, *The Guardian* newspaper claimed that the "high point of intellectual life on British television was the decade between the beginning of Channel 4 and the end of *The Late Show* in 1995". It was more than a coincidence that it was the era of Jackson's rise into the media arena and it seemed that he had the Midas touch.

He left *The Late Show* in 1991 to become the youngest Head of Department in the history of the BBC when he took over as television's Head of Music and Arts.

His star was in the ascendancy and in 1993, aged just 35, he became the second youngest Channel Controller in the BBC's history when taking over as Controller of BBC Two when Yentob moved to take over as Controller of BBC One.

In his three short years in control it was the only channel to actually increase its audience figures and a huge success for him was the decision, after almost ten years of previously aborted attempts, to bring to the screen the drama *Our Friends In The North*. It was eventually screened in 1996 after benefiting from a record budget for BBC Two of seven million pounds! The production earned a series of awards, BAFTAs from the British Academy Television Awards and from the Royal Television Society. Other huge successes were *This Life*, which ran from 1996-7 and the immensely popular *The X-Files* imported from the USA and shown from 1994-6. Jackson oversaw an excellent mix of drama, sci-fi, documentary and of course comedy. Hit shows *Ready, Steady, Cook*, which was first shown in 1994 and is still running today, the Esther Rantzen show, *Esther*, Steve Coogan's hugely successful comedy series, *Knowing Me Knowing You with Alan*

Partridge and the trend-setting fast moving comedy series, *The Fast Show* which ran from 1994-2000, were balanced by documentaries such as *The Death of Yugoslavia*. He was not averse to taking tough decisions such as closing down *The Late Show* in 1995 that despite contributing richly to his rapid rise through the ranks he now felt was too expensive for the present day market.

In 1996 John Birt instigated further changes at the BBC which resulted in Alan Yentob being appointed as Director of Programmes for BBC Production,not exactly a promotion, and Jackson was appointed to the dual role as Controller of BBC One and Director of Television responsible for all BBC broadcasting as well as the instigation and implementation of services designed for the coming digital television era. Many good judges surmised that Jackson had eclipsed his mentor. Perhaps as a response to the ruthlessness shown by the BBC's hierarchy, Jackson's tenure in his new role was to be extremely brief. He did launch a series of initiatives and one which has remained is the upgrading of the traditional BBC logo – a revolving world globe – replacing it with a hot air balloon in motion; not exactly revolutionary but it still survives.

However, the BBC was to suffer what one insider described as a hammer blow when, within twelve months of his appointment, Michael Jackson resigned from his post and in June 1997 took up the position of Chief Executive of Channel 4 in place of Michael Grade.

Unsurprisingly he could not resist the temptation of returning to a company, this time in complete control, that he was instrumental in establishing at the outset of his career.

Critics were generous in their praise and he was described as being "one of the best controllers the BBC has ever had".

He quickly made his mark when beating the BBC in a bidding war for the rights to show the England cricket team's home Test matches, a right that the BBC had held since 1938.There were many doubters, myself among them, who did not believe that Channel 4 could cope with Test Match cricket; well we were all proved wrong and in 2000, Channel 4's sports coverage team won a BAFTA for Best Sports Coverage.

The Channel underwent a strong revival; he was innovative and quirky, particularly with comedy and was not afraid to take risks with *Smack The Pony* (1999-2003), the way out *Da Ali G Show*, *So Graham Norton* (1998-2002), the sitcom *Spaced* (1999-2001) and *Black Books* (2000-04). His innovation and bravery were not to everyone's taste of course and he introduced (to me the awful but to many great) *Big Brother* series running from 2000. It was new and for many riveting television.

There was, however, criticism that in the field of drama he relied too much on American programmes that eventually proved too expensive. Nevertheless, his shrewd buys were box office successes, *Ally McBeal, The West Wing* and *Sex and the City* were all immensely popular. Perhaps in a step too far, he paid over one hundred million pounds for the rights to the American drama series *ER* together with, second time round, the sitcom *Friends*. He regretted and admitted the lack of home grown dramas but his tenure was not entirely devoid of British dramas as evidenced by *Queer as Folk* (1999-2000) and *Teachers* (2001-04). Jackson told an interviewer in 2001 that he regarded *Queer as Folk* as one of the 'signature shows' during his time at the station.

However, mistakes were made and there were budget problems created by the overspend on imported shows and the failure of the independent film production company, FilmFour Limited, established to make films and compete with the regular studios. Several films flopped leaving large losses to be accommodated and in 2002 the company was closed down and the channel reverted to the policy of backing films, as in previous years, such as *Four Weddings and a Funeral.*

Never one to let the grass grow under his feet the company launched successful spin-offs including the setting up of digital television channels E4 and Film4 both of which continued to thrive.

Despite even greater success in 2001 when Channel 4 won no less than eleven BAFTA awards, on 23rd July Michael Jackson dropped another bombshell when he resigned to accept an offer to work for Barry Diller's USA Entertainment company.

Jackson had rejected Diller in 2000 as he wanted to see to fruition the launch of the E4 digital channel but once that was done he believed that the time was ripe for yet another challenge. Once again he left a devastated team virtually at the top of their game and he was unquestionably a severe loss to Channel 4, who had shown a willingness to innovate and grow.

In the States Jackson's role was to be responsible for the cable television networks USA Network and Sci-Fi as well as overseeing the film company USA Films. After a series of mergers and reorganisation his role was defined as Chairman of Universal Television and he was responsible for the establishment of the successful series *Monk* in (2002-2009) and *The Dead Zone* (2002-2007).

In 2006 he took responsibility as, President of Programming, of Barry Diller's Inter Active Corp internet business, ensuring the production of multi-media features for the company's many websites.

At various times Michael Jackson's name has been linked with positions as vacancies have arisen at the highest level in the media world. It was rumoured that in 2002 he had applied for the role as head of the ITV network and it was surmised that he was a candidate for the post of Director-General of the BBC, following Greg Dyke's departure in 2004. In 2006 newspapers speculated that ITV wanted Jackson for the post of Chief Executive but Michael Grade got the job, but first of all he had to resign from his role as Chairman of the Board of Governors of the BBC.

Nevertheless despite the rumours there has been no news from Michael Jackson himself but, judging by his track record, it seems that he relishes new challenges and I am sure that we haven't heard the last of him.

Once again how fascinating to think that as we sit and watch some of our favourite programmes they may have been produced or bought by a fellow Maxonian for our entertainment.

The Arts, Business, Politics and Clergy

To stand out in the world of business and the arts the individual must have qualities that transcend the majority of the population. The gifts of flair and innovation, one can argue, are the principle requirements in a creative spirit and the same requirements are needed in the business world. The ability to recognise and identify detail and to turn the raw material into a picture, a story or a successful business requires not only skill but also hard work and determination.

There are several of our fellow citizens who have enjoyed those proven skills and who have been recognised at national level.

The Arts

Charles Frederick Tunnicliffe, OBE, RA, RE – Artist

Charles Tunnicliffe is recognised as not only one of the finest artists of his era but is regarded by the experts as being the leading wildlife artist of the twentieth century!

He was born in Langley village, Macclesfield on 1st December, 1901 to a father who was a shoemaker and a mother who was a farmer's daughter. Brought up on a farm in Sutton Lane Ends, he attended Sutton village school where the headmaster was quick to recognise Tunnicliffe's gift for drawing plants and animals. At the age of 14 and thanks to the headmaster, he entered the Macclesfield School of Art. However, one year later he enrolled at the Manchester School of Art which he attended from 1915-21. His talent received deserved attention and recognition and he won a Royal Exhibition scholarship to the Royal College of Art, where he met Malcolm Salaman who became his mentor and helped him in his first steps to becoming a printmaker. He left the Manchester Art School in 1925 and spent the next four years working as a part-time member on the staff at the Royal Society of Painter-Etchers and Engravers, where he was elected in 1929 as an Associate Royal Engraver. During this time he taught art and created etchings, particularly of farm animals and the Macclesfield countryside; he was beginning to create a reputation for himself.

However, his career direction was diverted in 1929 when, after marrying, he returned home to Macclesfield following the death of his father. For a time he worked as a freelance artist for several local companies with connections to the farming industry, creating etchings, paintings and printmaking. He started compiling an impressive series of sketchbooks replicating British birds in various stages of their life cycle and habitat. His reputation for immaculate detail was forged in these early sketches.

In 1932 came his big break when he was commissioned by Henry Williamson to make wood engravings to complement his hugely successful *Tarka the Otter* stories. The success of the whole venture made his reputation and ensured not only future commissions from Williamson but also requests to illustrate many other publications.

His fame and reputation continued to grow and, in 1934, he was elected Royal Engraver (RE) and commenced exhibiting his engravings at the Royal Academy. In 1938 he held his first solo exhibition at the Greatorex Galleries in London.

The Second World War was about to create havoc in the world and Tunnicliffe spent some time teaching art at Manchester Grammar School. It was during this time that he ventured into creating and writing his own books. One of his very best, *My Country Book*, was published in 1942, followed by a book dedicated solely to birds, *Bird Portraiture*, published in 1945. Just before the war ended he became an RA following his election in 1944 as an engraving associate of the Royal Academy. In 1945 he and his wife moved to the tranquillity of Anglesey, where his house Shorelands, at Malltraeth on the Cefni Estuary became the base and inspiration for some of his much loved later work. In particular perhaps his best work, published in 1952, was *Shorelands Summer Diary*, which reflected his present environment and the inspiration to continue to produce quality work on a subject that he had specialised in for many years – it had given him a fresh perspective.

Over his career Charles Tunnicliffe was much in demand as an illustrator, engraver and painter and has featured in more than 100 publications including many of the *Ladybird* book series. *A Book of Birds, The Seasons of the Woodman, Green Tide, Both Sides of the Road*, the list is endless, not withstanding many sketches for the Royal Society for the Protection of Birds (RSPB) and of course his own books. Experts regard his skill at drawing birds as being unparalleled in the art world and he was, of course, an accomplished painter in oils and watercolour as well as an engraver and printmaker. In short he was an artist without compare in his field. He was a most frequent exhibitor at the Royal Academy and achieved the ultimate accolade as an artist when, in 1954, he was elected a Royal Academician and in the same year was appointed Vice-President of the Royal Society for the Protection of Birds.

More honours followed when, in 1968, he was made Vice-President of the Society of Wildlife Artists and, in 1975, he received the gold medal from the RSPB. In 1978 he received an Order of the British Empire (OBE) for his services to the world of art.

He died at his home on Anglesey on 7th February, 1979.

There is a permanent exhibition of his work, oil paintings and etchings at the West Park Museum in Macclesfield.

The chances are if you see a superb drawing, engraving or painting of a bird in a quality gallery or book it will be by a local lad, Charles Frederick Tunnicliffe, OBE, RA.

Edith Maude Eaton – Author

If you have read any of the following short stories, articles and books, *Leaves from the Mental Portfolio of an Eurasian, A Chinese Ishmael, Mrs Spring Fragrance, Chan Hen Yen, Chinese Student, A Love Story from the Rice Fields of China, The Bird of Love* and *an Autumn Fan,* all written between 1896 and 1912 by Sui Sin Far in Canada and later in America, you would be astounded and forgiven not to be aware that 'Sui Sin Far' was the Chinese pseudonym, meaning daffodil, of Macclesfield born Edith Maude Eaton!

Edith was born in Upton, Macclesfield on 15th March, 1865, the daughter of a merchant Edward Eaton who had met his Chinese wife on a trip to Shanghai. His wife was the exotically named Grace 'Lotus Blossom' Trefusis who had been adopted by English missionaries.

Edith was the second oldest child of the fourteen children that eventually comprised the Eaton family. It was a considerable struggle for such a large family being raised at Upton Cottage, Upton. The family decided to emigrate and for a brief time settled in New York before moving to a more permanent base in Montreal, Canada. However, with many mouths to feed times were hard and poverty was ever present. Edith had to leave school early in order to help supplement the family finances. The family could not afford to educate their children in established facilities and began a home education programme. The parents clearly did an excellent job as Edith and one of her younger sisters Winifred both became successful writers.

Stimulated by her home environment and not subdued by it, Edith began to write even as a youngster and was almost immediately successful in having articles on the Chinese aspect published by both the *Montreal Star* and the *Daily Witness*.

Buoyed by her success she left home to work firstly in San Francisco, USA then in Seattle before moving east to Boston where she took work as a legal secretary.

She continued to write but strangely she concentrated, despite her typical, sedate, temperament and English mannerisms, on her Chinese background. She wrote from the viewpoint of a Chinese woman living in America and espoused the case for equal rights for Asian Americans in a fictional presentation but promoting the case for acceptance by American society. It was a brave approach and somewhat controversial as America had the Chinese Exclusion Act that ran from 1882 until 1943. She wrote under the pseudonym 'Sui Sin Far' ostensibly writing as a Chinese but spending her working days as a typical English woman.

She wrote her articles while working on a series of short stories that would eventually result in her first fictional novel *Mrs Spring Fragrance*, which was published in 1912.

She returned to Montreal where she died unmarried at the early age of 49 in April 1914.

An intriguing, unusual story of a Maxonian who crossed the world and enjoyed a dual identity to earn success.

Vera Brittain – Writer/Author
November 2008 saw the 90th anniversary of the ending of the First World War and as a result a collection of Vera Brittain's writings, particularly about the war, the part that women played in it and her own personal memoirs of a tragic time when not only her fiancé died but also her brother and two very close friends, were re-published in *A Testament of Youth*. In addition her book *Because You Died: Poetry and Prose of The First World War and After* was also re-issued and a television documentary was shown on BBC One, *A Woman in Love and War*, retelling her life story.

An educated woman, Brittain campaigned ceaselessly for women's rights and was an ardent peace campaigner, particularly after the horrors that she personally witnessed during the Great War. She was an outspoken feminist as well as a talented writer. Her daughter would become even more famous than her mother and just as outspoken attaining even greater renown for her political views, for her daughter is Shirley Williams, the Liberal Democrat peer and former member of the Labour Party for which she was once a Cabinet Minister.

Vera Brittain was born in Newcastle–under-Lyme on 29th December, 1893 to Thomas Brittain a wealthy paper merchant and Edith Bervon; shortly afterwards a son, Edward was born. The family moved to Macclesfield when Vera was just a few months old and lived at Glen Bank, a substantial white-painted semi-detached house with a large garden divided from a field by iron railings.

She had the advantage of being part of a wealthy family whose paper business was based in Hanley and Leek.

In her book *Testament of Youth*, she revealed that her family was very much middle class and recalled that Glen Bank had plush trappings, ornate heavy curtains, quality mahogany furniture, hunting pictures on the wall and engravings – typical of a well to do Edwardian family.

Her earliest memories of Macclesfield as a toddler involved crowds, noise, flags, banners and streamers as the town celebrated Queen Victoria's Diamond Jubilee and successes during the Boer War (1900-02). In particular she recalled an organ playing as crowds gathered in the decorated streets on a cold February morning to sing *We're soldiers of the Queen, me lad* and *Goodbye Dolly, I must leave you*, hugely popular patriotic songs of the time, declaring loyalty and love during a public celebration of the relief of Ladysmith. Her father took the family around the streets of the town by cab to witness the celebrations as the town went wild following the relief of Mafeking after a siege lasting more than 200 days.

When Queen Victoria died in 1901, Vera was drawing animals in the kitchen of the house when the cook read out the news, "The Queen is now asleep". She also remembers that, with her younger brother Edward, she started to cover the railings of the house with flags prior to the coronation of the new monarch but her father told her to take them down as the King to be was seriously ill. Vera recalled praying for him and was gratified when her prayers were answered; however her faith in prayer was not to last much longer.

She was fortunate to live in a middle class environment detached from the poverty around her and with the enviable fortune to be taught at home by AM Newby, a governess, as well as the attention and service from a housekeeper, a cook and two maids.

Her father was outspoken and firm in his views and visitors to the house, apart from relatives and close friends, were few and far between. Vera recalled and it is a reflection perhaps of her own later prejudices and the influence of her father, that the personalities of the people of Macclesfield and later Buxton were typical of a small town – she implied boring. Wives kept house, husbands, if bank managers, were cautious and un-enterprising, solicitors were safety first types unwilling to take a risk, as were most businessmen, and doctor's bedside manners camouflaged their lack of diagnostic abilities; her father banned schoolmasters from the house as he found them too boring!

There was however always music in the house and sometimes her mother would stage musical evenings when she would sing. There were pianoforte solos and sometimes Vera and her brother Edward, at the ages of nine and seven, would play duets and would form a trio when joined by their governess.

Strangely, given her future life, there was little literary interest apart from the basic children's fairy tales of the time. Despite this deficiency Vera nevertheless had a taste for writing and began to write her own stories at the age of five. She was however searching for influences and was first inspired at the age of eight when she discovered books in the house, Longfellow's *Complete Poems* and Mathew Arnold's *Sohrab and Rustum*. She read them avidly and was able to quote from them. Her mother eventually responded and brought literature to her family on Sunday afternoons when she would read Charles Dickens to Vera and Edward. Throughout this time Vera's mind was set on writing and with the help of her governess, who obtained paper for her from local Macclesfield mills, she wrote a series of five novels called The Dicks and every night at bed-time she would read from them to Edward

At the age of 11 she left Macclesfield but years later recalled the garden at Glen Bank and the pretty Cheshire hedgerows, lanes and wildflowers and was grateful that Macclesfield had been a haven for her serene and privileged upbringing. Certainly it was at Macclesfield that she first revealed, and started to hone, the literary skills that would later earn her everlasting fame.

Her primary education and her formative years were spent in Macclesfield before the family moved to Buxton to enhance the children's education and then later Vera was sent to be privately educated at a boarding school in Surrey.

She said in her book that from a very early age she noticed and resented the inequality between the sexes. Although she adored and was very close to her young brother she resented the obvious preferential treatment that he received from time to time principally because of his gender; she would spend her lifetime fighting for equality.

Her father was a man very much of the old school and did not appreciate his intelligent daughter's desire for education, believing that a woman's main role in life was marriage. Vera's persistence wore him down and when she qualified for university he gave his permission to attend Sommerville College, Oxford in 1913.

At Oxford not only did she achieve her desire for education but she also met, fell in love and became engaged to Roland Leighton, a fellow student and a close friend of her brother Edward. However the First World War was about to erupt and Roland and Edward joined the army and Vera left Oxford to join a Voluntary Aid Detachment (VAD). The family home was still in Buxton and Vera would return home from time to time. She remembered a moment when war was deemed to be imminent returning with her parents by car to Macclesfield to obtain cheese, bacon and butter to store, fearing a shortage of food supplies. Macclesfield was clearly remembered for its shopping facilities!

Vera was single minded and her decision to join VAD was no empty gesture. She was determined to play her part and, while her men-folk were fighting, she attended the wounded in England, Malta and France. It was during the dreadful tasks that she had to perform that her lifetime opinions were formed.

The war claimed her fiancé, her beloved brother and several close friends. She herself wrote later about the filth, the gore, rotting corpses, the sheer horror of mustard gas on the human body and of having to attend the wounded and the dying enveloped by intense cold, bloodied tables and bandages, the stench of death all around them and their only means of coping was a "pair of forceps standing in a potted meat glass half full of methylated spirits".

This total waste of human lives, she wrote in her book, was far from the glamour associated with the original call to arms requested by the politicians.

At the end of the war a shattered Vera returned to Oxford to continue her studies where she met Winifred Holtby, a woman who would become her friend for life.

In 1919 Vera had her first success when *Verses of a VAD*, including a poem as a tribute to her late brother, was published. She continued to study at Oxford and graduated in 1921 with Winifred and they moved to London where they hoped to become writers.

Vera had two novels published: *The Dark Tide* was published in 1923, and attained a level of notoriety because it contained critical comments on sexism at Oxford University, and in 1925 *Not Without Honour* was published, sadly neither book was regarded as successful. She was, however, also working as a journalist and had more success in that genre, writing in particular for the feminist journal *Time and Tide*. She continued however to write books and two more came off her production line, *Women's Work in Modern Britain* published in 1928 and *Halcyon of the Future of Monogamy* published in 1929. Her political views were changing and she moved from the Liberal Party to Labour and for a time nurtured the desire to become an MP. However romance returned to her life and she married George Catlin, an American academic and went to live in America where she eventually gave birth to her children John in 1927 and Shirley in 1930. Sadly it was not to last as she missed England so much and took the decision to return home where she lived with her old friend Winifred Holtby.

Vera then embarked on what was perhaps her most successful period as a writer and a pacifist,being strongly involved with the, Peace Pledge Union. In 1933 she wrote her most famous book *Testament of Youth*, an autobiography containing details of her growing up in Macclesfield, her struggle for education and her First World War experiences as a nurse; it became a bestseller in Britain and America. During this time she was indebted to her friend Winifred, who it was believed brought up Vera's children during this very hectic time. Winifred died in 1935 and Vera's next bestseller *Testament to Friendship* was dedicated to her relationship with her.

As the Second World War loomed she became more and more active with the peace movement and at times was regarded as unpatriotic with her journal *Letters To Peace Lovers*; she had witnessed the horror and did not relish the idea of a repeat. Two more books were published criticising various elements of government policies.

After the war she continued to write promoting women's issues including *Lady into Women*, a history of the women's movement, a second part of her autobiography *Testament of Experience* and *Women at Oxford* published in 1960.

In 1957, still pursuing her ideals she joined the Campaign for Nuclear Disarmament (CND) and lined up alongside, JP Taylor, Michael

Foot, Bertrand Russell, Kingsley Martin, JP Priestley and many others, and was still active in the movement until her death in Wimbledon on 29th March, 1970.

Her ashes were scattered, in accordance with her wishes, on her brother's grave where he was killed and buried in Italy.

An old saying states, "give me the child at seven and I'll give you the man" – if that really is the case then Vera Brittain was 'made' in Macclesfield.

It was reported in the *Daily Telegraph* in February 2009 that BBC Films intended making a film of her life based on her book *Testament of Youth*. It may not be too long until once again the film cameras invade Macclesfield in celebration of one of its famous citizens.

Business

James Brindley – Canal Engineer

Macclesfield has a tenuous claim on Britain's foremost canal engineer, who from an early age was a gifted engineer that could fix and build almost anything. He became a millwright in Leek, owning his own business in his mid 20s, and in 1752 designed and built an engine used for the vital operation of draining coalpits. However, his love of building steam engines was supplanted when he discovered his gift for building canals. At the time it would become the greatest, easiest and most economical way to travel and transport goods around the country. He was responsible for constructing Britain's first major canal, the Bridgewater Canal completed in 1765, whose major purpose was to transport coal from Worsley to Manchester a distance of ten miles. His fame and reputation established, he went on to construct the Trent and Mersey Canal and the Staffordshire and Worcester Canal. In all it is believed that he was responsible for establishing and constructing in total over 360 miles of canals, easing communications and transportation and helping facilitate the dawning of the Industrial Revolution.

He was born in Wormhill, Buxton in 1716 to James and Susannah Brindley and was taught to read and write by his mother. However, although he was regarded as semi illiterate he quickly discovered his gift for making things work. His connection with Macclesfield came when he went to work as an apprentice millwright to Abraham Bennett at his mill in Sutton, Macclesfield. It was during this time he was called out to Macclesfield in 1735 when a severe fire at the button factory of

Daintry & Ryle on Park Green damaged much of the machinery. The young Brindley, he was about 19, set about trying to restore order to the chaos. It was a testimony to his talents when the machinery was once again up and running.

Brindley spent more than seven years in Macclesfield as an apprentice before leaving to start his own business as a millwright and then on to the history books as Britain's first and acknowledged greatest canal engineer.

He died on 27th September, 1772 leaving behind a widow, two daughters and a son from whom Arnold Bennett the writer descended.

Charles Roe – Industrialist

It was Charles Roe who was largely credited with starting Macclesfield on the way to world recognition as a silk producer when he established the first silk producing mill in the town, using water to power production. Although he is always associated with the silk industry he was also very much involved in mining and the metal industry, particularly copper.

He was born in Castleton, Derbyshire on 7th May, 1715 to a local vicar the Reverend Thomas Roe and Mary, his wife, and was the youngest of eight children. He came to Macclesfield following the death of his parents, to live with family, when he was about eight years old. Although it cannot be confirmed, it is believed that he was educated at the Macclesfield Grammar School (King's School).

As a youngster he had every intention of entering the Church, perhaps persuaded by the fact that his father had been a vicar and two of his brothers had also devoted their lives to the Church. However, family problems thwarted Roe's ambition and he entered the textile industry in the town. After a very successful period as a businessman in the button and twist industry he became a Freeman of Macclesfield in 1742.

In 1743, inspired by the discovery in Italy by John Lombe of the value of water power in the silk throwing process, Roe built a small mill powered by the water from the river at the bottom of Mill Street/ Park Green: the site is today commemorated by a small plaque.

In the same year he married Elizabeth Lankford with whom he had three children. He was a highly influential person in the town and was made mayor in 1747 and by the end of his year of office, buoyed by the success of his mill on Park Green, he had built an even larger mill on Waters Green purely for the production of silk, entering into partnership with Glover & Co.

The Roe family resided in what is today known as Charles Roe house a well-preserved elegant old house, on the corner of Chestergate/Churchill Way that is still in use today.

Sadly his wife Elizabeth died in 1750 and in 1752 Roe married Mary Stockdale, by whom he had eight children before her premature death in 1763.

Roe was by now a wealthy man but was not the type to rest on his laurels and, in 1756, commenced a copper mining operation in nearby Alderley Edge and another in the Lake District at Coniston. Happy with the copper extraction element of the business he needed a smelting operation and established a site on the Macclesfield Common using coal from a local mine.

Roe went on to build rolling mills in Eaton, Congleton and Bosley for brass-wire as his business interests diversified. In 1763 he decided to stop buying copper ore and extended his mining operations to North Wales and then, in 1764, obtained a long lease to extract ore from Parys Mountain in Anglesey and started to extract lead from a mine in Caernarvonshire.

top: *Site of the first silk factory in Mill Street/Park Green*
above: *Charles Roe House, Chestergate*

In 1766 he married Rachel Harriott with whom he had a son and as his business empire expanded he opened copper-smelting facilities, firstly in Liverpool and then at Toxteth Park. Soon after, he took over a coal colliery in Wrexham and managed to organise the transportation of the coal and the ore to a specially built small dock close to the smelting works at Toxteth.

In 1768 a massive lode of copper ore was discovered at his Anglesey mine that resulted in it becoming the largest copper mine in the whole of Europe. The discovery came at just the right time for Roe as his company ceased to mine at Alderley Edge and later, in 1770, at Coniston, as the remaining deposits became harder and therefore more expensive to extract.

His business interests continued to prosper and in 1774 in conjunction with a number of partners, he formed the Macclesfield Copper Company, which became one of the greatest and biggest producers of brass in Europe towards the end of the century.

Roe also produced his own coinage; penny and half penny tokens used to pay the workers in Liverpool, Bosley, Congleton and Macclesfield. The coins were inscribed 'Macclesfield' and around the edge stated, 'Payable at Macclesfield, Liverpool or Congleton'. However, in 1797, the production of such coins was made illegal and over the ensuing years have become collectors items.

The legacy of Charles Roe to the town of Macclesfield is highly visible: Roe Street, Charles Roe House in Chestergate, the site of his first silk mill at Park Green, but above all the highly distinctive building Christ Church that Roe dedicated to the people of the town.

The town had grown considerably following the explosion of the silk industry and was recognised in Britain and Europe as one of the great silk producing centres. The growth in the silk industry, as well as making Roe a wealthy man, had put a strain on the town's resources. But not only did Roe give land to the Corporation to assist with the need for extra burial spaces but he set about building a new church with the intention of providing space for at least 1,000 worshippers. The work was started in the early part of 1775 and finished towards the end of the year at a total cost estimated at around £8,000. The distinctive tower together with bells was added in 1777 and the building was consecrated and named Christ Church in 1779. It was Charles Roe's gift to the town and somehow made up for his thwarted ambition to dedicate himself to the service of the church.

He is commemorated in the Church with a copy of an oil painting of himself and, on the south wall of the church, there is a tribute to the man and his achievements: a cogwheel, a bust of himself and reliefs showing Christ Church, his Park Green Silk Mill complete with waterwheel and a depiction of his Liverpool copper smelting facility complete with billowing chimneys. In the grounds of the church there once stood the Roe family vault, a sixteen-foot tall pyramid shaped monument, that is now sadly dismantled. However, the West Park Museum features his life and deeds and acknowledges the great contribution to the town of one of the foremost industrialists of his time.

Charles Roe was unquestionably a skilled entrepreneur with remarkable vision and in many ways well ahead of his time. Silk, copper, coal and brass were the keys to his success but he was also a great benefactor to the town and the people of Macclesfield. He appreciated his wealth and success and was modest over his considerable achievements.

He died on 3rd May, 1781 and was buried in the family vault in the churchyard. His third and last wife Rachel also died in 1781.

Christ Church, built 1775

Sir John Henry Birchenhough, Ist Baronet, GCMG
A Maxonian with the rare and distinctive honour of a bridge named after him in Africa, is one of this country's most honoured and decorated businessman.

Henry Birchenhough, born in Macclesfield on 7th March, 1853, was the second son born to John Birchenhough, a silk manufacturer who was mayor of Macclesfield in 1876, and his wife Elizabeth formerly Taylor. The family lived in some style in a grand house in Great King Street.

He grew up supported by his wealthy family and studied at Oxford University, spending part of his education in London and later Paris before returning to Macclesfield to participate in the family silk business.

The family was well connected and shortly after the end of the South African War it was suggested by Lord Milner that Birchenhough be sent to South Africa as a Special Trade Commissioner responsible for the establishment of trade between the two countries. From 1897 until around 1902 he wrote a number of articles for the *Nineteenth Century Magazine* on a variety of trade topics: *Do Foreign Annexations Injure British Trade, England's Opportunity, The Expansion of Germany, The Future of Egypt, The Imperial Function of Trade, Local Beginnings of Imperial Defence, A Business View Of South African Pacification, Mr Chamberlain as an Empire Builder* and *Preferential Tariffs within The Empire*, displaying an intellectual insight and a prophetic vision of what was to come.

Unsurprisingly, the highly regarded Birchenhough was successful and his efforts gained him the recognition of an appointment as a Companion of the order of St Michael and St George (CMG). As trade became established, Birchenhough's reputation continued to grow and, in 1905, he became a director of the British South Africa Company.

Although his business life was hectic and the recognition warming he found time to marry Mabel who was a daughter of the Very Reverend George Granville Bradley, the Dean of Westminster, and together they raised two daughters.

After giving first class service over a number of years and being highly influential in Africa he was knighted in 1916, Knight Commander of the Order of St Michael and St George (KCMG) for his services to Rhodesia.

However, in 1906 the much in demand Birchenhough was appointed to the Royal Commission on Shipping Rings and was also a member of the Advisory Committee to the Board of Trade. Throughout the First World War he worked with the Board of Trade and then afterwards he chaired the committee appointed by the Board of Trade to consider the position of the textile trades post-war, a position for which he was well suited. He also worked closely with the Ministry of Reconstruction and received full recognition for his contributions when he was created a Baronet in the New Years Honours list of 1920.

In 1925 he was appointed president of the British South Africa Company, a position he was to hold until the end of his life.

More honours came his way when, in 1935, he was promoted to Knight Grand Cross of the Order of St Michael and St George (GCMG). He was also chairman of the Beit Railway Trust from 1931-37, a company that was instrumental in constructing the Birchenhough Bridge over the Save River in Rhodesia now, of course, Zimbabwe.

After his death on 12th May, 1937, his ashes were interred in a pillar on the bridge named after him over the Save River in Zimbabwe.

Sadly Birchenhough had no male heir to succeed him so the baronetcy died with him.

Kenneth Culley – CBE

Born on 3rd June, 1942 in Collar House, Prestbury to parents James and Lily, Ken grew up in Preston Street, Macclesfield in modest circumstances. Lily was a domestic help and Ken's father, James would tackle virtually any job to provide for his family: at times he worked as a dyers labourer, worked in the brewery industry, became a chimney sweep and also turned his hand to repairing shoes, as a cobbler.

Ken's early education was at Duke Street Primary School where his ability rewarded him with a place at King's School.

After leaving King's he joined AP Smith Atkins & Co, where he trained as an accountant, before leaving the firm to join the Cheshire Building Society in 1961.

In 1964 Ken married Barbara May Hooley but sadly, although the marriage would be blessed with two daughters and a son, they divorced in 1982.

While establishing his career ambitions, Culley was very much into local sport and played soccer with Hurdsfield Rovers, with life long friend Nemmie Jones, and also played with Macclesfield Wednesday. He reminds me that he had to negotiate his Wednesday afternoons off to play soccer as part of his holidays. He also played cricket, as I did, with Maxonians (King's School old boys) and with the occasional appearance with Macclesfield Nalgo.

In 1965 he left the Cheshire Building Society to take up the post of accountant at the Bradford and Bingley Society. After four years gaining valuable experience, in 1969 he returned to the Cheshire as Assistant Secretary and was later appointed General Manager, a position, despite its title, signifying that he was second in command.

The Cheshire Building Society grew to be a solid and powerful institution but Ken was ambitious to take the next step and to be in control. In pursuit of his ambition he resigned from the Cheshire in 1983 to become the Chief Executive of the much smaller Ramsbury Building Society, with the avowed intent of making it bigger than the Cheshire. 1983 was a pivotal moment in Ken Culley's life; he married Pamela and left Macclesfield for the last time to pursue his ambitions.

In time, after a number of mergers, and the acquisition of some smaller societies and a change of name to the Portman Building Society, Ken Culley built the former Ramsbury Building Society up from a £125 million base to over £7 billion to become the fourth largest building society in the country. In 1999 he took the decision to take early retirement after a job well done. Ken was saddened by the eventual takeover of the Portman by the Nationwide in 2007 that resulted in the loss of the jobs of several of his old colleagues and friends.

During his time overseeing the growth of the Portman, his abilities attracted attention and he was appointed to serve on a number of national bodies. From 1995-97 he was a Director of the Building Societies Trust, was elected to serve on the national Council of the Building Societies Association (effectively the BS trade union) and was appointed chairman in 1995; in 1998 he was appointed Deputy Chairman of the International Union of Finance Institutions but his early retirement from the industry precluded his appointment to the Chair.

In 1998 he received the ultimate accolade for his services to his industry when he was awarded the Commander of order of The British Empire (CBE).

Having retired after a high profile career, Ken's experience attracted offers of non-executive roles from a number of companies and he has served as Chairman of JP Morgan Fleming Elec plc, Chairman of Marks and Spencer Financial Services and is a Director of British Insurance plc.

Ken told me, during my research, that although he is settled in the south he still returns home to visit family and friends and attends board meetings in Chester twice a year. He is also an avowed supporter of Manchester City and a season ticket holder.

He lives today in Berkshire and has the interest and enjoyment of six grandchildren, two of whom, twin boys, share his support of Manchester City. Ken also enjoys the tranquillity of his garden and fishing.

In those seemingly carefree days of laughter and fun at King's School who could have forecast the solid base that was being created.

Peter Ellwood, CBE

One day in 1989, in my capacity as Area Director for TSB for the North West based in Liverpool, I was invited to Manchester to have lunch with my new boss Peter Ellwood, the recently appointed Chief Executive of Retail Banking. I was unaware of his background details, apart from the fact that he had enjoyed a high profile banking career with Barclays from whom he had recently departed.

Over an enjoyable lunch I discovered to my amazement that he was an old boy of King's School, knew Macclesfield well and indeed his time at the school (1954-61) had encompassed my own time there. Alhough I did not remember him (he was younger than me) but he kindly said that he remembered me. I suppose that as I was older and a member of the cricket First Eleven and had won a boxing championship my profile was slightly elevated!

He was an easy conversationalist, astute and aware, and over the next few years I grew to recognise his ability and on the few occasions that we met we had the opportunity, rare as it was, to reminisce about our schooldays.

Peter Ellwood was not Macclesfield born; in fact, he was born on 15th May, 1943 in Manchester to parents Isaac and Edith Ellwood. At the age of 9 he moved with his family to High Lane near Poynton. He meets the qualifications for this book because from the age of 11 to 18 he was educated in Macclesfield, travelling to the King's School on a daily basis from 1954-61.

After leaving school he joined Barclays Bank in Bristol, at the age of 18, and after attaining his banker's qualifications he became a Fellow of the Chartered Institute of Bankers (FCIB). He moved through the ranks and eventually attained the exalted position of Chief Executive of Barclaycard, a post he held from 1985-89 until he left to join the fast changing and growing TSB Bank as Chief Executive of Retail Banking.

As the bank started to embark on an active expansion programme, he found himself appointed in 1992 as Group Chief Executive of The TSB Group and two years later he was also appointed Chairman of Visa International until relinquishing the post in 1999.

TSB started to expand, merging with Lloyds Bank, taking over the Cheltenham and Gloucester Building Society and later purchasing the Scottish Widows organisation. In 1997 Peter Ellwood found himself Chief Executive of Lloyds TSB Group plc, at the time Britain's largest bank, a position he held until his retirement in 2003.

Peter Elwood, CBE

In 2001 he also became the first chairman of Employers for Work-Life Balance, a position he held until stepping down in 2007. Also in 2001 he received the accolade for his service to banking when he was awarded the Commander of the Order of the British Empire (CBE).

One would think that a period of rest and recreation would follow retirement, spending time particularly with wife Judy Ann, whom he married in 1968, and their three children. However in 'retirement' he has held the post of Deputy Chairman of ICI plc, taking over as Chairman in 2004 until the company was sold to Akzo Nobel in 2008. During this time his services were sought by Prime Minister Tony Blair who asked him to lead the Race Equality and Diversity Task Force at the Institute of Public Policy Research think tank.

No sooner had he stepped down from ICI than he was appointed Chairman of the Rexham Group plc, the world's largest can manufacturer!

His interests are music and the theatre; he is a non–executive director of the Royal Philharmonic Orchestra, Deputy Chairman of the

Royal College of Music, President of the Northampton Bach Choir and a trustee of the Royal Theatre, Northampton. If all that were not enough, he is also Chairman of the Royal Parks Charitable Foundation as well as the Royal Parks Advisory Board.

Since his retirement Peter somehow found time to return to the King's School, Macclesfield where he gave a career talk on banking drawn on his own experiences. It would be difficult to find a more perfect example of a local lad reaching the very top of his career, culminating in becoming the boss of Britain's largest bank.

Politics

Rt Hon Sir Alan James Beith, MP

Alan Beith was born in Poynton on 20th April 1943 to parents James and Joan. He was educated from 1954-61 at the King's School, Macclesfield (another class mate of mine) travelling daily from his Poynton home. Alan was not, I remember, outstanding on the sports field but was regarded by his fellow students as an academic, preferring study to sports activities.

Even in his early teens he was interested in social and political issues and for a time he was a sub-editor on the local *Poynton Post* before leaving King's School for Oxford University.

After leaving Oxford he took up the appointment of lecturer at Newcastle University, a position he held from 1966-73.

In 1965 he married Barbara Jean Ward and together they had a son and a daughter. Alan was anxious to get into politics and had an early opportunity when, in 1970, he stood as a parliamentary candidate for the Liberal Party in the General Election (he was 27), contesting the seat at Berwick upon Tweed. He was unsuccessful, finishing third, but it was valuable experience and three years later he contested the seat again and triumphed by 57 votes. Since that triumph in 1973, Sir Alan Beith has represented the Liberals in parliament and enjoys the status of being the party's longest serving member of parliament.

At the age of 33 he became the Chief Whip of the party, a post he held from 1976-85 when he relinquished it to take up the prestigious role of Foreign Affairs spokesman. His stature grew rapidly within the party and in 1985 he became Deputy Leader of the Liberal Party.

However, there followed a traumatic time when the party started to implode and a new party emerged from the old and, in 1988, the Liberal Democrats Party was born. Alan Beith became the Treasury

Sir Alan James Beith, MP

spokesman from 1988-94, then in 1994 he was appointed Home Affairs spokesman but relinquished that position, in 1997, to become the spokesman on Home and Legal Affairs.

From 1992 until 2003 he combined his several changes of office with the prestigious role of Deputy Leader of the Liberal Democrats. Although this period in his life was productive in the career sense it was personally a terrible time. His wife Barbara died in 1998 and then his only son died in 2000. It was a time of tragedy and for Alan, who was also a Methodist Preacher in his locality, it was a time for calling on his inner strengths and receiving comfort from his beliefs.

Speaking in the House of Commons

Although his constituency is many miles from London he prides himself on always being available when required by his constituents and conducts open surgeries each month in Alnwick and Berwick. When he gets any spare time he enjoys walking, boating and music. In 2001 he found happiness when marrying Baroness Maddock.

In the House of Parliament he makes himself known on a whole variety of topics, never selling his constituents short on issues that he believes are important to him and the people he represents – he will always stand on principle. In 2008 he refused to serve on an all-party committee looking into the police 'invasion' of Parliament in their search for information about an MP. He believed that the committee was being 'interfered' with by the government and he refused to be part of it.

In December 2008 his service to politics was recognised when he was knighted by the Queen in a ceremony at Buckingham Palace. He told the press afterwards "It was a very special occasion for me and my family and we will treasure the memories for a long time. I was very pleased indeed to have had the knighthood conferred by her Majesty".

Hard to reconcile the young lad I knew more than 50 years ago with the hardened skilled politician kneeling before the Queen to be knighted; arise Sir Alan James Beith.

Rt Hon Sir Nicholas Winterton, MP

Sir Nicholas Winterton does not qualify for inclusion amongst famous Maxonians for he is not Macclesfield born, raised or educated and neither does he live in the town. However, since 1971, he has represented the constituency from his home in Mow Cop, near Congleton, for nigh on four decades and is one of the longest serving parliamentarians in the House of Commons. A Conservative, he has proven to be a vociferous and energetic representative of all the town's people.

Born on 31st March, 1938 in Longden Green, Rugeley, Staffordshire he attended Bilton Grange Preparatory School and later Rugby School before starting his working life in industry. Soon he was turning his attention full time to politics where he quickly made his mark with several localised appointments.

He married Jane Ann Hodgson in 1960 and was successful in his second attempt to enter Parliament in 1971, when replacing Air Commodore Sir Arthur Vere Harvey as MP for Macclesfield. My mother was housekeeper to Mrs White, who was a former chairman of the Macclesfield Conservative Party, and helped organise and host Winterton's introductory function.

Over the years, in the House of Commons, he was respected for his outspokenness, refusing to indulge in party politics and firmly representing the people of Macclesfield, not just the conservative party. Many believe that if he had been more subservient he would have attained higher office.

Nevertheless respect within the House of Commons has led to his inclusion in many all-party committees on a whole range of issues.

From 1991-92 he chaired the government's Select Committee on Health; from 1985-2005 he was an additional Deputy Speaker in Westminster Hall and for more than twenty years (1973-99) he has been a National Advisor on the Duke of Edinburgh Award Scheme Committee as well as being a regular member of the Speaker's Panel and a member of the House of Commons Chairman's Panel.

His service to British politics was recognised when in 2002 he was knighted by Her Majesty the Queen.

He has displayed over the years an indefatigable commitment to the Macclesfield community, with an interest in local bodies too numerous to list.

He is a Freeman of the City of London and in 2002 was made an Honorary Freeman of the Borough of Macclesfield. In 2008 there was some controversy over the treatment of his personal benefits through allowances and expenses but an enquiry revealed that nothing illegal had taken place.

His wife, Lady Ann Winterton entered politics after raising her four children and became the Member of Parliament for Congleton in 1983. In 2009 Sir Nicholas and Lady Winterton jointly announced that they would be stepping down at the General Election in 2010 in order to spend more time with their family.

Author's Note: I first met Sir Nicholas Winterton when I was Chairman of Macclesfield Forest Round Table and he was a top table guest and fellow speaker at our annual dinner in 1974. Over the years I had contact with him through Round Table charitable activities and he was always good humoured, self-deprecating and supportive of our efforts to raise money for local needs.

Clergy

Macclesfield can lay claim to the two most high profile clerical figures of the twentieth century.

Hewlett Johnson – Dean of Canterbury, The Red Dean
Hewlett Johnson was a highly controversial figure, who at various times, was on intimate terms with some of the most famous and infamous historical figures of modern times. He spent his formative years and his early education at Macclesfield Grammar School, in time King's School, but later in his life he met and befriended TS Eliot, Sybil Thorndike, Paul Robeson, President Trueman of the USA, Nikita Khrushchev and Malenkov – both of whom would serve as Premiers of the Soviet Union, Ghandi, Chinese leaders Mao Tse Tung and Chou En-Lai, who loaned Johnson his private plane, Josef Stalin – President of the Soviet Union, President Sukarno of Indonesia, Cuban President Fidel Castro and British Prime Minister Ramsay MacDonald. He could never have imagined, as he studied in the peace and calm of Macclesfield, that one day he would meet the leaders who would shape the history of the world during the twentieth century, as well as receiving from Stalin, in the Kremlin in 1945, the 'Order of the Red

Sir Nicholas Winterton, MP

Banner and later in 1951 he uniquely received, also from Stalin, The Stalin Peace Prize, the equivalent of the western world's Nobel Prize. Also, even more uniquely, he was awarded the Mongolian Star for his peace efforts.

He was born in Kersal near Manchester on 25th January, 1874 to Manchester wire manufacturer Charles Johnson and wife Rosa; he had two brothers and three sisters. Macclesfield Grammar School was at the time, one of the most renowned schools for excellent education standards. The good and the wealthy sent their children there to study and for most to reside in live-in accommodation. Hewlett Johnson came to know Macclesfield very well during his formative years before eventually leaving King's School in 1890 or 1893 (accounts vary) for Owens College, Manchester where he obtained a BSc in Civil Engineering. He was intent on a career in engineering and won a geological prize and in 1898 became an associate member of the Institute of Civil Engineering. However, influenced by friends, he turned to socialism and in 1905 graduated in theology from Wadham College. His life was also shaped by meeting Mary Taylor, the daughter of a wealthy merchant, and after marrying her in 1902 and graduating in theology, he entered the church and became ordained before accepting a curacy at St Margaret's, Dunham Massey, near Altrincham, where he was made vicar in 1908.

Outspoken in pursuit of his social ideals with very strong, often radical views and supported by Mary he worked ceaselessly to improve life for his parishioners. For example, the Johnson's were the first to organise holiday camps for the poor and he was vociferous in his pursuit of better housing for the working class. Typically he was unconcerned that the residents of his wealthy parish were often upset by his outspokenness. It was an attitude that would govern the rest of his life. Mary ran a hospital for soldiers injured in the First World War and for a time Johnson was chaplain to a German prisoner of war camp; they had also visited Germany, just after the war and it was these experiences that directed Johnson into the path of pacifism.

From 1905 to around 1925 he ran a much-respected religious publication, *The Interpreter*, providing a forum for open opinions on the bible.

Prime Minister Ramsay MacDonald appointed Johnson Dean of Manchester Cathedral in 1924 and he instigated changes that are current even today. He opened the church to everyone all day and actively encouraged children to attend. After travelling extensively in Europe he returned, determined to improve sanitary and habitat (for example, cleaner air) for all and continued his campaign for better housing and working conditions for the working class.

His work and reputation were gaining momentum when tragically in the early part of 1931, Mary died of cancer. Triumph however followed tragedy when later that year he was appointed to the much-coveted post of Dean of Canterbury Cathedral.

He now had an even larger platform to express his religious and ever increasing political views that often set him at odds against the accepted role of the church and government. His responsibilities were heavy in running the largest and most highly regarded Church in the Christian faith but he still found time to travel extensively and to expound his views on social inequalities and pacifism.

In 1932 came perhaps the pivotal period in his life when he travelled throughout an almost lawless China, through Tibet and Mongolia and, despite continual dangers, he sent reports back to the British press. He became highly impressed with the small but growing band of communists who were trying to change matters in China for the poor and oppressed. The mission was fraught with danger, with stark living conditions and in no way could be regarded in the same light as today's pampered political 'junkets'.

On his return to Canterbury he continued with his work and politics and became friendly with the Russian Ambassador and met Gandhi when he visited the cathedral. In 1937 Johnson spent three months in Russia and when he returned to England he was asked to write an explanatory book on Russian Communism to help put over the ideal to the British public. In 1938 Johnson married Nowell Edwards, a cousin's daughter, who in 1936 had also spent some time touring Russia. Just before the book *The Socialist Sixth of the World* was published in 1939, Johnson wrote an article, *Act Now. An Appeal to the Mind and Heart of Britain*, outlining the cases of fascism and socialism and propounded that the Russian way was the way forward.

The Second World War defused a lot of the growing antagonism toward Johnson and his views but in 1940 a number of the clergy wrote to *The Times* disassociating themselves from his views and Field Marshall Montgomery visited Hewlett Johnson to try to ascertain from him Russia's strengths.

After the war Johnson toured Russia and during the massive VE Day celebrations in Moscow, *The Times* reported "Students gathered outside the hotels where diplomats and foreign visitors were staying. A short while ago they were carrying shoulder high the Dean of Canterbury."

The Dean continued his tour of Russia and on 6th July was summoned to the Kremlin and presented by Stalin with the Order of the Red Banner of Labour, a great honour. To counter balance his views he was invited to America in 1945 and 1948, to the increasing annoyance of the Archbishop of Canterbury who was becoming irritated by Johnson's political reputation over his role of promoting the church.

Undeterred, Johnson continued and now in his mid seventies he toured Australia and spoke at peace rallies in Czechoslovakia and

Poland. In 1951 he was guest speaker at the World Peace Conference in Berlin. Back home, however, opposition to his political views was growing and there was a concerted attempt to have him ostracised from the church – hoping to force his resignation.

The whole situation was compounded when, in 1951, Hewlett Johnson attained the rare distinction of being awarded the Stalin Peace Prize, akin to the awarding of a Nobel Prize in Western Europe, receiving the award from Stalin at the Kremlin. He also received a congratulatory letter from Soviet Premier to be, Nikita Khrushchev.

The award ceremony, where he was surrounded by his Russian friends, was regarded almost as treachery by much of the British public as the 'cold war' with Russia had intensified. There were many who believed that Johnson's ego was being polished and that he was being used as a political pawn.

The British press referred to him as 'The Red Dean' indicating that he was a communist sympathiser. However, he continued with his travels to Hungary, Romania and Bulgaria and three visits to China in the 1950s where he was feted by Mao Tse Tung and given the use of Chou En-Lai's personal plane. A visit to Mongolia resulted in him receiving that country's highest honour, the Mongolian Star.

In 1952 the Archbishop of Canterbury signed a motion in the House of Lords authorising the dismissal of Johnson as Dean of Canterbury but Johnson's supporters defeated it and once again he survived.

Nevertheless, opposition to him intensified when Russia invaded Hungary in the late 1950s and Johnson refused to condemn the invasion. Thick skinned or downright awkward, the Johnson's later attended the fortieth anniversary celebrations of the Russian October Revolution.

Incredibly, in his late eighties, Johnson continued his world travels and in 1961 approaching his 88th birthday he engaged in a television debate, called *Head On*, with aspiring young politician, Jeremy Thorpe.

In 1962 at the age of 88, weakened by an accident and continual argument, Hewlett Johnson finally resigned as Dean of Canterbury after more than thirty years in office.

Even after retirement he made another controversial decision and attended the fiftieth anniversary of Cuban Independence following a personal invitation from Fidel Castro. In his 90th year he made his last visit to China and on 22nd October, 1966 at the age of 92 died of pneumonia. Despite the many years of controversy he was buried in the Cloister Garth of Canterbury Cathedral.

Regarded by many as a 'traitor' Hewlett Johnson, despite his notoriety, was basically a good man at heart and a good Christian who strived to right social inequality and was concerned about the poor and the working class. He was unquestionably stubborn and strong willed but perhaps politically naïve, and was clearly used by the communist world for propaganda purposes as they saw in him a high profile advocate of their way of life.

Terence Hardy Waite, CBE, MBE

During the late 1980s and until his release in November 1991, Terry Waite dominated the headlines of the world's press when he was kidnapped and taken hostage by Shiite Muslims in Lebanon and literally disappeared off the radar. During his ordeal he had the dubious distinction of becoming the world's longest detained hostage. He was born on 31st May, 1939 in Bollington, Macclesfield to Thomas William Waite, a police constable and Lena Hardy and lived in the police house in the centre of the village.

His mother recalled that it was after they moved to Henbury when Terry was only a toddler that he first took an interest in the church that was a five-minute walk from where they lived. An elderly neighbour had started to take Terry to church and one day he was particularly late and when Terry heard the sound of the church bells he set off and entered the church on his own: he was barely five years old.

The family eventually moved to Styal near Wilmslow and Terry was educated at Wilmslow School and Stockton Heath.

The family were soon on the move again, this time to Thelwall, and at the age of 16 Terry started work in Warrington. Surprisingly he wanted to join the army and enlisted in the Grenadier Guards at the age of 17. However, his army career was cut short, due largely to an allergic reaction believed to have been caused by the dye used in the uniforms. During this time his earlier interest in the church resulted in him regenerating that interest and he enrolled at the Church Army College in London and became a student of theology.

The Waite family were not particularly religious and believe that Terry's interest was self-generated, so much so that he was the youngest person to receive a Sunday school prize. Perhaps his values were inherited from his father who was regarded as a firm but warm disciplinarian, renowned for his conscientiousness, and more concerned with the reasons why offences were committed preferring to help people rather than condemn them. These standards were very

Terence Hardy Waite, CBE, MBE

much a part of Terry Waite's qualities as his career progressed in the Anglican Church.

In 1964 he married Helen Frances Watters and also in that year he received his first appointment as lay education advisor to the Anglican Bishop of Bristol.

His talents were quickly recognised and he moved with his family to Uganda to work with the Anglican Archbishop of Uganda, Rwanda and Burundi. In 1972 he worked for a time in Rome and then in the USA before settling down in London around 1978. In 1980 he was appointed assistant to Archbishop Runcie of Canterbury and was quickly elevated onto the world stage when he was sent as the Archbishop's special envoy to negotiate the release of hostages taken in Iran in 1981.

In 1982 his work was recognised when he was awarded the Member of the British Empire (MBE). In 1984 his expertise was once again required and he spent several months negotiating and gaining the confidence of Colonel Gadhafi in order to successfully obtain the release of more hostages. Further recognition and appreciation came when the BBC made him 'Man of the Year' for 1985.

His skill at negotiating and arbitrating were to plunge him into an almost five year nightmare when he was appointed by the Archbishop of Canterbury, Robert Runcie to be his representative and visit Lebanon, in 1987, to negotiate the release of a number of western hostages being held by the Shiite Muslims. Lebanon was engaged in a virtual civil war, with the country in chaos, and Waite was warned of the dangers beforehand.

Whilst on his way to a meeting with the Shiite's he was taken hostage along with his driver who was later released unharmed.

From 2nd February, 1987, he was held prisoner in desperate and trying conditions being moved from house to house to avoid detection. Often he was chained to radiators and virtually starved with no contact with any outsiders until well into his detention. The kidnappers threatened execution and for a time promised release and then prevaricated, rejecting all humanitarian pleas from the outside world. Waite had come under a truce banner agreed by both parties and was to all intents and purposes an innocent bystander. It was a terrible time for his family, wife, three daughters and a son who daily were kept in suspense.

Eventually on 17th November, 1991, he was released and news of his freedom was broadcast around the world. In 1992 he was awarded the Commander of the British Empire (CBE) and also received from America, the Franklin D Roosevelt Freedom Award.

After his release Terry Waite became a regular guest on television and radio programmes and has written many articles as well as books: *Taken on Trust: An Autobiography* published in 1993, *Footfalls in Memory: Reflections from Solitude published in 1997 and Travels with a Primate: Around the World with Archbishop Robert Runcie* published in 2000, as well as being the subject of a number of books. He has a number of honorary degrees and is a member of a whole range of charitable bodies and social organisations including a Vice Presidency of the East Cheshire Hospice, Macclesfield.

He lives in Cambridge and much deserves the peace and tranquillity to indulge in his hobbies of music and travel.

On 12th March, 2009 Terry Waite returned to the area to give a talk *An Evening With Terry Waite* at the Tytherington Club, Macclesfield.

In June of 2009, following the announcement that the long serving MP Sir Nicholas Winterton intended to stand down at the next General Election, there was speculation that Terry Waite may contest the seat as an Independent. He told the press "I know the area well; it has an important place in my heart because I spent my formative years here. I'd love to live in Bollington again". He went on to explain that if he did stand for election "It would be for the people, and I'm not seeking power or glory".

Later, despite the conjecture, Waite decided not to stand. A world-renowned figure much admired and respected who first saw the light of day in the small village of Bollington.

Acknowledgements and sources

A work such as this, requiring personal detail of many people over a considerable period of time, requires thorough research, fact finding and confirmation of facts over the fanciful. I am indebted for the input from the following organisations and publications:

Canadian Aviation Hall of Fame
Cheshire Life
King's School Former Pupils Association (JM Spencer Pickup)
Macclesfield Express
Oxford Dictionary of National Biography
The Independent Newspaper
Wikipedia

108 Steps, Around Macclesfield by Andrew Wild. Sigma Press
A History of Macclesfield by C Stella Davies. Manchester University
    Press
Manchester, A Celebration by Brian Redhead. Andre Deutsch Ltd
Memoirs of a not so Dutiful Daughter by Jenni Murray. Bantam Press
The Spirit of Macclesfield by Doug Pickford. Landmark Publications
Streets/Houses of Old Macclesfield by John Earles. MTD Rigg
    Publications
Taken on Trust by Terry Waite. Hodder & Stoughton General Division
Testament of Youth by Vera Brittain. Virago Press.
Touching from a Distance by Deborah Curtis. Faber & Faber

My thanks also to the following individuals:
Steve Mellor, Dr Mike Dexter, Helen Atkinson Wood, Geoff Lloyd, Benedict Allen, 'Lord' Tim Hudson, Chris Nicholl, Mrs Diana Millett, Mrs Valerie Brown, Mrs Donaldson, Mrs Margaret Armitage, Terry Louden, Ken Whittaker, Ron and Joan Swindells, Derek and Margaret Way, Sheila Mason, Joyce Holland, Nigel Robinson and Mike and Myra Clarke.

Also from Sigma Leisure:

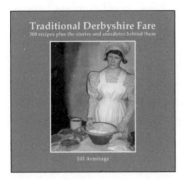

Traditional Derbyshire Fare
300 recipes plus the stories and anecdotes behind them
Jill Armitage

Some Derbyshire dishes are well known, like the Bakewell Pudding; many more, including some of the most delectable, are little known outside the places whose name they bear. The recipes are individual, easy, economical, with readily available ingredients, and have a strong regional accent. This is Derbyshire food at its best.
£12.95

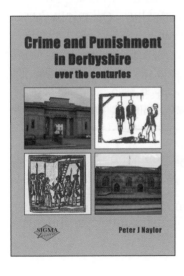

Crime and Punishment in Derbyshire over the centuties
Peter J Naylor

Crime fascinates us all, particularly murders, and the bloodier they are the better they are received. It would appear that the Peak District was a lawless place until more recent times. This book is a thorough mix of most of the types of crimes committed in Derbyshire over the centuries. Each chapter is dedicated to a different type of crime and the punishments handed out. Whilst this book gives much of its space over to murder, other crimes are also included.
£8.99

Rocky Rambles in The Peak District
Fred Broadhurst

"The Peak District has a dramatic story to tell and Fred Broadhurst is just the guide we need." – Aubrey Manning, presenter of the BBC TV series 'Earth Story'.

You don't have to be an expert or even an amateur geologist to enjoy these 'rocky rambles'! Where better than in and around the Peak District would you find geology right there beneath your feet - all you need to know is where to look.

The comprehensive glossary of terms, which covers the identification of Peak District Rocks, forms an invaluable supplement and provides 'at a glance' information for the reader.

£8.95

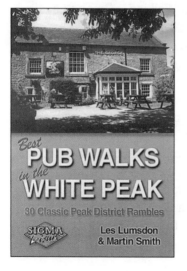

Peak District Walking – On The Level
Norman Buckley

Some folk prefer easy walks, and sometimes there's just not time for an all-day yomp. In either case, this is definitely a book to keep on your bookshelf. Norman Buckley has had considerable success with "On The Level" books for the Lake District and the Yorkshire Dales.

The walks are ideal for family outings and the precise instructions ensure that there's little chance of losing your way. Well-produced maps encourage everybody to try out the walks - all of which are well scattered across the Peak District.

£7.95

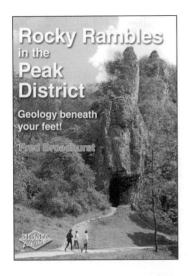

Rocky Rambles in The Peak District
Fred Broadhurst

"The Peak District has a dramatic story to tell and Fred Broadhurst is just the guide we need." – Aubrey Manning, presenter of the BBC TV series 'Earth Story'.

You don't have to be an expert or even an amateur geologist to enjoy these 'rocky rambles'! Where better than in and around the Peak District would you find geology right there beneath your feet - all you need to know is where to look.

The comprehensive glossary of terms, which covers the identification of Peak District Rocks, forms an invaluable supplement and provides 'at a glance' information for the reader.

£8.95

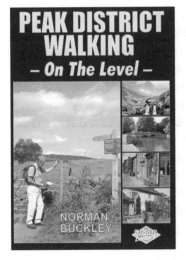

Peak District Walking – On The Level
Norman Buckley

Some folk prefer easy walks, and sometimes there's just not time for an all-day yomp. In either case, this is definitely a book to keep on your bookshelf. Norman Buckley has had considerable success with "On The Level" books for the Lake District and the Yorkshire Dales.

The walks are ideal for family outings and the precise instructions ensure that there's little chance of losing your way. Well-produced maps encourage everybody to try out the walks - all of which are well scattered across the Peak District.

£7.95

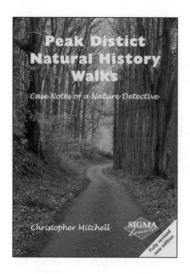

Peak District Walking Natural History Walks
Christopher Mitchell

An updated 2nd Edition with 18 varied walks for all lovers of the great outdoors — and armchair ramblers too! Learn how to be a nature detective, a 'case notes' approach shows you what clues to look for and how to solve them. Detailed maps include animal tracks and signs, landscape features and everything you need for the perfect natural history walk. There are mysteries and puzzles to solve to add more fun for family walks — solutions supplied! Includes follow on material with an extensive Bibliography and 'Taking it Further' sections.

£8.99

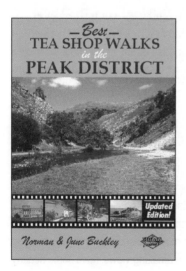

Best Tea Shop Walks in the Peak District
Norman and June Buckley

A wonderful collection of easy-going walks that are ideal for families and all those who appreciate fine scenery with a touch of decandence in the shape of an afternoon tea or morning coffee —or both! The 26 walks are spread widely across the Peak District, including Lyme Park, Castleton, Miller's Dale, and The Roaches and — of course — such famous dales as Lathkill and Dovedale. Each walk has a handy summary so that you can choose the walks that are ideally suited to the interests and abilities of your party. The tea shops are just as diverse, ranging from the splendour of Chatsworth House to more basic locations. Each one welcomes ramblers and there is always a good choice of tempting goodies.

£7.95

Derbyshire Walks with Children
William D Parke

There are 24 circular walks, ranging from 1 to 6 miles in length, and each one has been researched and written with children in mind. The directions and background information have been checked and revised as necessary for this updated reprint.

Detailed instructions for parents and an interactive commentary for children mean there's never a dull moment. There are even 'escape routes' to allow families to tailor each walk to suit their own needs, time and energy.

"The needs, entertainment and safety of children have been of paramount importance."
– Peak Advertiser
£7.95

All-Terrain Pushchair Walks: The Peak District
Alison Southern

The Peak District, in the heart of the country, has some of England's most picturesque landscapes, from the White Peak in the south with its rocky outcrops and steep hills, to the Dark Peak in the north with peat moss moorland and stunning vistas. This book is for families with all-terrain pushchairs and buggies, and for everyone wishing to avoid as many stiles and obstacles as possible. Includes family-friendly attractions, trees to identify, birds and plants to spot, and lots more to discover. Have fun while you walk enjoying the amazing views, have some healthy exercise and spend time with the family away from the modern world.
£7.95.

Peak District Trigpointing Walks
Hill walking with a point to it!
Keith Stevens & Peter Whittaker

A superb introduction to an intriguing new walking experience: searching out all those elusive Ordnance Survey pillars. Packed with detailed walks to new and interesting Peak District summits, with a wealth of fascinating information on the history of the OS and the art of GPS navigation.

There are 150 Peak District Ordnance Survey pillars — can you find them all? Walk to all the best scenic viewpoints — from the top you can spot all the surrounding pillars. This book shows you how. £8.95

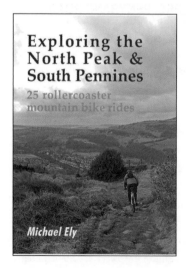

Exploring the North Peak & South Pennines
25 rollercoaster mountain bike rides
Michael Ely

This book will inspire you to pump up the tyres and oil the chain for some excitement, exercise and a feast of rollercoaster riding as you join Michael Ely on some great mountain biking in these Pennine hills. Over 500 miles of riding for the adventurous off-road cyclist that explore the tracks and steep lanes in the Pennine hills. There are twenty-five illustrated rides - with cafe stops half way round - to provide both a challenge and many hours of healthy exercise. £8.99

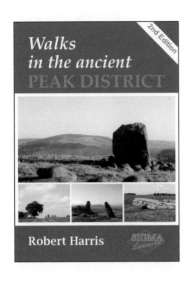

Walks in the Ancient Peak District
Robert Harris

A collection of walks visiting the prehistoric monuments and sites of the Peak District. A refreshing insight into the thinking behind the monuments, the rituals and strange behaviour of our ancestors. All the routes are circular, most starting and finishing in a town or village that is easy to locate and convenient to reach by car.
£8.99